THE
GLORIOUS
YEARS

THE
GLORIOUS
YEARS

MAGAZINE

Materials © Emap Active Limited 2007
Compilation and cover design © Haynes Publishing 2007

First published in 2007

A catalogue record for this book is available from the British Library

ISBN 978 1 84425 430 9

Published jointly by
Haynes Publishing, Sparkford,
Yeovil, Somerset BA22 7JJ, England
Phone 01963 440635,
www.haynes.co.uk
And
Emap Active Limited,
Wentworth House, Wentworth Street,
Peterborough PE6 1DS, England
Phone 01733 213700.
www.emap.com

Produced for Haynes Publishing and Emap Active Ltd by
Black Cat Graphics, Black Cat House, Freestone Road,
St. Philips, Bristol BS2 0QN. England

Printed and bound in England by

J.H. Haynes & Co. Ltd, Sparkford
The authors and publishers (Emap Magazines and Haynes Publishing) have taken care to
ensure that the advice given in this book is current at the time of publication; however they
will accept no liability for any economic loss, damage to property or death and personal
injury arising from it other than in respect of injury or death resulting directly from their
negligence. The reader should take account of the circumstances and consider carefully the
appropriateness of any practices or techniques mentioned, and any information or
instructions provided, and seek further guidance or expert assistance as necessary.

Contents

Foreword

Welcome to 'The Glorious Years', a collection of the finest photographs to have graced the pages of *Steam Railway* magazine in recent years. Steam locomotives, and the steam age railway, are intensely photographic subjects: the exhaust from hard working engine on a crisp winter's day, the fire, the smoke, the movement of the engine itself and its interplay with the landscape around it... steam railway can form stunning images

Ever since its inception in 1979, *Steam Railway* has been a forum for the very best steam pictures, both the conventional and more avant garde.

Long-running features such as 'The Glorious Years' (featuring working British steam before it finished on BR in 1968) and Gallery - the best of steam today - have become institutions. That's been down purely to the dedication, skill and enthusiasm of the hundreds of photographers who contribute to the magazine. It's in large part due to them that *Steam Railway* has been the world's biggest selling steam magazine from the start.

Many photographers think nothing of driving hundreds of miles just to get one picture. Others go to extraordinary lengths to recreate scenes from 40 or more years ago. Yet others will trek around the world to hunt out the very last steam locomotives still working for their living, to capture them on film before it's too late.

This book is about the steam engines, but it's a tribute to the photographers and their pictures. Thanks to all of them - and we hope you enjoy this 'Gallery of Steam'

Tony Streeter
Editor, Steam Railway

The publisher would like to acknowledge the diligent efforts of Susan Voss, Mel Holley and the staff of Emap Licensing for making this project possible.

Hugh Ramsey

■ What started your interest in railways?
My mother took me to New Southgate station in the summer of 1947 when I was 12 years old. I remember walking down the wooden stairs to the platform as 'Pacific' No. 112 *St Simon* raced through heading south. From then on I was hooked and I became a regular at New Southgate.

■ How did you start out in railway photography?
I started with a Kodak folding camera in the 1950s, and the results just magically take me back to those days. Later on I spent my savings on a Voightlander camera (in 1961) which I mainly used to record the East Coast scene between then and 1963.

■ Do you have any regrets?
Yes, I regret never going round the South Wales locomotive sheds. Living on the Great Northern we would never dream of travelling over to South Wales!

■ Where was your favourite location?
The Great Northern main line was my favourite location and still is now. I stayed local to the line I was born with - I lived close by. Saturday afternoons saw us going further afield on our bikes to Cricklewood, Neasden, Willesden (where we would often see the new '76XXXs' ('4MTs') for the Southern Region before they were delivered) and finally to Old Oak Common. I also became a regular visitor to Swindon, making the trip about once every fortnight for a time. When we arrived the group was told to stay together, but once inside we had the run of the works, particularly on Sundays.

■ When did your Glorious Years come to an end?
To a degree they have never stopped. I still go out photographing steam, diesel and electric traction, including recording the last days of the '86' electrics on the West Coast Main Line. But the 1950s were my real Glorious Years and I treasure those days - I have every moment written down in diaries. In August 1968 we genuinely did think it was the end of steam on BR. But when *King George V* returned to the main line in 1971, that was another Glorious Year.

Left: The Midland and Great Northern Preservation Society special on May 27 1961 took LMS Ivatt 'Mogul' No. 43151 to Wisbech. In a scene full of wonderful period detail, the 'Flying Pig' runs round the train, which had originated at Peterborough North. No. 43151 was a familiar engine in these parts - it had entered traffic 10 years before at Melton Constable. By this time it was based at New England (Peterborough) after which it moved to Barrow Hill on March 3 1963, a roundhouse currently enjoying a preservation renaissance.

The fireman of GWR 'Castle' No. 7036 *Taunton Castle* leans out as the four-cylinder 4-6-0 powers away from Swindon on September 10 1961. *Taunton Castle* was the penultimate 'Castle' built, completed on August 17 1950 to Collett's design. At the time of the picture the double-chimney 4-6-0 was allocated to Old Oak Common, from where it was withdrawn in the week of September 7 1963. Nowadays it is not only the works that has gone or been turned to other uses - Swindon station has also been rationalised since this photograph was taken.

Above: The 'A' shop touch - WR 'Manor' No. 7825 *Lechlade Manor* sparkles alongside Swindon's famous 'Factory' traverser on September 24 1961. The locomotive's last overhaul before withdrawal (from Reading on May 11 1964) has just been completed. 'A' shop is now as much a memory as *Lechlade Manor* but the traverser survives, at the Flour Mill in the Dean Forest (SR268).

Above: Scottish Veteran - just over a month after withdrawal (on March 12), Pickersgill 4-4-0 No. 54466 is already showing the signs of inactivity at Inverness MPD on April 21 1962. These elegant Caledonian Railway 4-4-0s were introduced in 1916. Construction continued until 1922 by which time 48 locomotives had been built. Withdrawal was spread out over a decade - the first was withdrawn in 1953 and the last went in 1963.

Above: World record holding LNER 'A4' No. 60022 *Mallard*
stops at Doncaster with a Retford-Blackpool 'Northern Rubber
Special' on September 30 1961. In comparison to *Mallard*'s
1938 feat the highest recorded speed on the run was sedate -
72 mph at Black Carr Junction, before Doncaster. Later in the
tour the train would tackle Copy Pit with banking assistance
from 'WD' 2-8-0 No. 90348. *Mallard* was allocated to 'Top
Shed', Kings Cross and was withdrawn on April 25 1963. It is
now on display in the National Railway Museum, York. Steam
still uses the East Coast Main Line, and even, occasionally, the
climb to Copy Pit.

Right: Perfect portrait: Holden 'J17' 0-6-0 No. 65567 basks in
the sun at Thetford on March 31 1962 having brought in the
RCTS tour from Norwich Thorpe. No. 70003 took over here for
the return to Liverpool Street (see pic left). 90 'J17s' were
built between 1900 and 1911. No. 65567 was built in 1905 and
so was a real veteran by the time it was withdrawn on June 8
1962. Sole survivor No. 65567 (as LNER No. 8217) is part of
the National Collection, on display at York.

Above: On the same day, Collett 2-8-0 No. 3859 stands on Swindon shed, before returning to its home MPD at Pontypool Road. Its last general overhaul before withdrawal (on May 21 1965 from Southall) has - like that of *Lechlade Manor* - just been completed. The GWR's 'Heavy Freight' 2-8-0 design dated back to 1903, although the later Collett engines had detail differences including side-window cabs. Nine '2884s' have survived along with seven of Churchward's '28XXs'.

Left: Work-worn 'V2' 2-6-2 No. 60939 stands on shed at King's Cross, along with a 'Pacific', on February 11 1962 waiting for its next duty. The Gresley 2-6-2 was a York North engine and was never based at 'Top Shed'. The 'V2s' were introduced in 1936 and a total of 184 were built for express passenger and freight traffic. Withdrawal for No. 60939 came on October 12 1964 from York North. No. 60800 is preserved at York.

Above: LNER 'B1' 4-6-0 No. 61303 stands out from its grimy stablemates at Bridlington MPD on
August 6 1961. The other locomotives include grubby 'K3/3' 2-6-0 No. 61883, and unidentified members of both classes. No. 61303
was a Thornaby engine and later moved on to Hull Dairycoates and York North, before withdrawal on November 21 1966.

Above: Steam enthusiasts young and old line the track at Thetford as sparkling 'Britannia' No. 70003 *John Bunyan* waits to take over the RCTS Great Eastern Commemorative Steam Railtour from 'J17' No. 65567. It's March 31 1962 and GE steam was to end that September. No. 70003 was withdrawn from Carlisle Kingmoor on March 25 1967, after just 15 years in BR service.

Bottom Left Opposite: Memories of North London: Kentish Town (14B), February 11 1962... Stanier 'Black Five' 4-6-0 No. 44853 potters around the deserted yard of the former Midland shed. Allocated to Holbeck at the time, No. 44853 lasted a further five years before withdrawal for scrap, being sold to Cohen's of Kettering. At Kentish Town in 1962 however, the 'Five' seems in fine fettle...

Above: Arthurian sunset: No. 30782 *Sir Brian* takes a break at Ramsgate on an LCGB railtour to mark the end of steam on the SR's South Eastern Division. The tour, on February 25 1962, ran from Victoria to Margate, Ramsgate and New Romney. The 'King Arthur' ran from Victoria to Ashford where an even more geriatric 'C' 0-6-0 took over until New Romney, before a 'Schools' returned the train to Charing Cross. *Sir Brian* had just seven months to go before withdrawal - by the end of September it had been cut up at Eastleigh.

Above: Gresley 'A4' No. 60030 *Golden Fleece* races through Hatfield on April 14 1962 with a fast freight during its last months on the East Coast Main Line. The 'A4' was allocated to Kings Cross, one of only two sheds the 'Streak' had been based at since nationalisation (the other was Grantham). No. 60030 was withdrawn on December 29 and later ran light to its Doncaster birthplace for breaking up.

Left: The RCTS 'Border Rail Tour' of July 9 1961 took NBR 'D34' 4-4-0 No. 256 *Glen Douglas* and LNER 'J37' 0-6-0 No. 64624 from Hawick to St Boswells, Greenlaw and Roxburgh Junction where they have backed off the train. *Glen Douglas* was built at Cowlairs in 1913 and at the time of the railtour was officially stored. It was withdrawn on December 17 1962 and is now preserved at the Bo'ness and Kinneil Railway.

Right: Polished LNER 'A3' 4-6-2 No. 60061 *Pretty Polly* stands at 'Top Shed' (34A) on February 11 1962, between lines of grime-encrusted goods locomotives including a 'WD' 2-8-0 and a '9F'. In the background a new 'Deltic' gives a splash of modernity, whilst awaiting its next duty.

Pretty Polly was allocated to King's Cross between November 8 1959 and June 16 1963. The 'Pacific's' final shed was Grantham, from where it was withdrawn on September 16 1963.

Above: One of 70 '61XX' 2-6-2Ts, No. 6141, stands under the train shed at Paddington with passengers looking on in the early to mid-1960s. The high-pressure boiler gave the class, built between 1931 and 1935, greater haulage capacity for the empty stock workings into Paddington. The boilers were rated at 225psi (in comparison with the similar '5101' 2-6-2Ts which had 200psi). The locomotive was withdrawn in December 1965 from Gloucester shed. One of the '61XXs' survives, No. 6106, which is based at Didcot.

Alistair Nisbet

■ What started your interest in railways?

Railways have always been part of my life. Until I was three we lived in Fife, about 100 yards from the railway. The line was mainly worked by ex-North British Railway 'C16' 4-4-2Ts on 'locals' while through trains to
St Andrews and Edinburgh saw ex-NBR 'Scott' and 'Glen' 4-4-0s plus a few GCR-style 'Directors'. Peter Poundtext, Jingling Geordie and Kettledrummle went hand in hand with Laird of Balmawhapple and Ellen Douglas. After the Second World War my father's employer sent him to work in London. At first we lived in a flat overlooking the Northern Line's Morden car sheds, before we moved to Sutton. I travelled to school by train and it was a natural progression to do the same when I started work.

■ How did you become interested in railway photography?

Travelling to work in Central London for seven years I saw a wide variety of locomotives between Wimbledon and Waterloo. The 'Lord Nelson' and 'King Arthur' 4-6-0s had already gone and the 'M7' 0-4-4Ts and 'Schools' 4-4-0s were disappearing. So I bought myself a small 35mm camera (from Werra with a Zeiss Tessar lens). My present collection is all Olympus kit - an OM4, OM1 and three OM40s.

■ Where was your favourite spot for photography?

Many pictures were taken on my travels between Wimbledon and Waterloo, and being a season ticket holder it cost nothing to go out at weekends. However I had two other areas which I preferred, mainly for the peace and quiet. The first was the Guildford to Redhill line with its hourly service of 'N' and 'U' 2-6-0s plus the occasional BR or GWR interloper. I held a trackside pass for this line.
I also enjoyed being back in Fife to see my Grandmother. The railway to Tayport was still there, albeit only with a local service from Dundee Tay Bridge using 'Standard
4' 2-6-4Ts and
occasional 'B1' 4-6-0s.

■ What was your approach to photography?

 Without making a conscious decision to do so, I was recording the daily scene as I found it, often from station platforms but also from the trackside or overbridges, and even occasionally from train windows. I rarely visited sheds but do have shots taken at Nine Elms on the final day of SR steam, plus a few taken at Dundee and Perth and on visits to Willesden and Neasden.
The bulk of my pictures were taken on monochrome - FP3 and Adox KB17 (anyone remember that?) I developed them myself in the kitchen and printed them in a darkroom at work. I spent one evening a week there but even so I estimate about half the 6,000 negatives I took then have never seen an enlarger.

■ When did your Glorious Years come to an end?

 July 1967 at the end of Southern steam - soon afterwards I was married and we moved to Ipswich, which had already been a steam 'desert' for six years. Nevertheless, I did go to Manchester for the specials in August 1968 and even persuaded my wife Jenny to come to see the famous '15 Guinea Special' - sitting up all night too. We stayed on at Victoria deciding what to do after 4-6-2 No. 70013 Oliver Cromwell had left, and were fortunate to see the 'Black Five' which had brought the train from Liverpool making its way back through the station - hardly anyone was about by then. These days I take mainly landscapes and set subjects for camera club competitions but occasionally I do go out in the Banbury area, and I took the club to the Severn Valley Railway at the end of June.

Above: Charging round the curve out of Tayport, BR 'Standard 4' 2-6-4T No. 80123 heads the 8.6am train to Dundee Tay Bridge in July 1964. The area around the Tay Bridge was where Alistair Nisbet grew up, and he subsequently visited every year. The Standard tank, one of 155 constructed between 1951 and 1957, was built at Brighton in 1955. It was withdrawn on January 30 1966 and sold to Shipbreaking Industries for scrap.

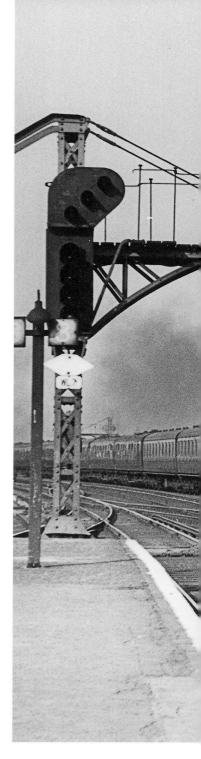

Above: Steam enthusiasts young and old line the track at Thetford as sparkling 'Britannia' No. 70003 *John Bunyan* waits to take over the RCTS Great Eastern Commemorative Steam Railtour from 'J17' No. 65567. It's March 31 1962 and GE steam was to end that September. No. 70003 was withdrawn from Carlisle Kingmoor on March 25 1967, after just 15 years in BR service.

Bottom Left Opposite: Go south for sunshine... Station staff busy themselves unloading the guard's compartment as 'Standard 3' 2-6-2T No. 82027 backs down on to the lunchtime Wareham-Swanage train on May 15 1964. The Swanage branch – now the Swanage Railway – still sees plenty of steam, but not '3MTs'. No. 82027 was withdrawn in January 1966. The Swanage Railway was reopened in sections from 1975, after closure in 1972, and now has a connection to the main line at Wareham again, although it is not yet in use.

Above: With locomotives passing through every minute, Clapham Junction was 'locospotter' heaven'. On August 17 1963, after a summer shower, the driver of Bulleid 'Battle of Britain' No. 34090 *Sir Eustace Missenden* opens up the regulator while in charge of the 8.22am London Waterloo to Bournemouth West. The rebuilt 'Light Pacific' survived another four years in service - it was withdrawn from Eastleigh on July 9 1967, the final day of Southern steam.

Above: The size of Perth station can be appreciated in this view from the bridge as 'Britannia' No. 70011 *Hotspur*, allocated to Carlisle Kingmoor, sets out with the 'Fish' to London's Broad Street from Aberdeen on July 15 1964. The BR 'Pacific' was built in 1951 and lasted just 16 years in traffic before being withdrawn. In its short lifespan it was allocated to four different sheds. *Hotspur's* final depot was Carlisle Kingmoor, to which it moved from Upperby shed in December 1965. It was withdrawn in 1967.

Left: The impending end of steam still seems far away at Bournemouth on August 5 1963. Whilst a Bulleid 'Pacific' waits on a through line, 'Standard 4' 2-6-0 No. 76064 moves off shed ready to take over a 'stopper' for Weymouth. The third rail has yet to reach Bournemouth and semaphores still proudly guard the station. It is a classic Southern scene, for now at least!

Right: In a scene evocative of the end of Southern steam, BR 2-6-2T
No. 82019 rumbles out of London Waterloo station on April 4 1967
between two generations of EMUs, just three months before the end
of steam on the Southern Region. On the right, the Maunsell 4-COR
unit, built in 1937, is almost twice the age of the 'Standard 3', yet
outlasted it. No. 82019 only entered traffic in 1952 and was
withdrawn in 1967. The 4TC unit on the left was built to replace
steam, coinciding with the completion of the Bournemouth
electrification.

Right: Twilight of the gods. Southern steam is into its last weeks as No. 35023 *Holland-Afrika Line*, with steam oozing from every pore, starts away from Waterloo on March 31 1967. *Holland-Afrika Line* had moved to Nine Elms from Weymouth just five days before. But the last day of Southern steam was by now four months away. *Holland-Afrika Line* was there at the end – on July 9 1967.

Below: Go south for sunshine... Station staff busy themselves unloading the guard's compartment as 'Standard 3' 2-6-2T No. 82027 backs down on to the lunchtime Wareham-Swanage train on May 15 1964. The Swanage branch – now the Swanage Railway – still sees plenty of steam, but not '3MTs'. No. 82027 was withdrawn in January 1966. The Swanage Railway was reopened in sections from 1975, after closure in 1972, and now has a connection to the main line at Wareham again, although it is not yet in use.

Above: BR 'Standard 3' 2-6-2T No. 82024 leaves Kensington Olympia on August 8 1965 for Clapham Junction. Olympia is still a hub of activity even though the locomotives and rolling stock have changed over the years. No. 82024 was built in 1954 and first allocated to Exmouth Junction. The 2-6-2T was withdrawn from Nine Elms on January 30 1966.

Above: The now-preserved 'M7' No. 30053 (currently out of ticket at the Swanage Railway) takes water at Brockenhurst on the Southampton to Bournemouth line on May 15 1964. The Drummond-designed 0-4-4T, built in 1905 at Nine Elms, has just arrived with the shuttle from Lymington Pier, a service which is still operated today, by South West Trains EMUs. No. 30053 was withdrawn in 1964 from Bournemouth shed. It is one of only two 'M7s' in preservation - the other is No. 30245, based at the National Railway Museum in York.

STEAM
RAILWAY

Above: Once this was a common sight all over the country - one of 733 Riddles 'WD' 2-8-0s, No. 90628, rumbles across the Tay Bridge with up coal empties. It is June 21 1965 and No. 90628 is allocated to Thornton Junction, its last shed. A reminder of the Tay Bridge disaster lurks in the water that laps at the piers of the two-mile long bridge. The footings of the original bridge, which collapsed in 1879, are still in place - as indeed they are today.

Ron Sewell

■ What started your interest in railways?
Undoubtedly it was steam that caught my imagination. There was a holiday we took by train to Ilfracombe probably in 1947 or 1948 of which I remember nothing, but I do remember visiting some of the London termini and two pictures at Waterloo in 1954.

■ How did you become interested in railway photography?
Watching my father take pictures and seeing the results naturally led to my following his example. In fact, I photograph other subjects besides railways, but it was inevitable that I should try my hand at railway photography. Photographers like Eric Treacy and Ivo Peters were a source of inspiration.

■ Where was your favourite spot for photography?
Living in London did not offer exotic locations. The Clapham Junction area including Vauxhall station was the most frequently used, but the Marylebone and Euston lines were often visited and were nearer home.

■ What is your approach to railway photography?
My approach is 'pictorial' wherever possible, but having no control over lighting, steam and smoke often means a 'record' picture results!

■ What was your favourite locomotive class?
The rebuilt Southern 'Merchant Navy' 4-6-2s, hence my membership of the Merchant Navy Locomotive Preservation Society (keepers of No. 35028 Clan Line, currently under overhaul).

■ When did your 'Glorious Years' come to an end?
For me it was in June/July 1967. In June there was a run from Penrith to Crewe with Stanier 'Black Five' No. 45347 (at Crewe one of the new electric locomotives took over) and a trip to Bournemouth behind No. 34001 Exeter.
Then in July 1967 I made a brief evening visit to Waterloo where I found a filthy, No. 35030 Elder Dempster Lines, minus nameplates and with the number painted on the smokebox. Even now I can remember how depressing it seemed.

Left: You can almost hear LMS 'Patriot' 4-6-0 No. 45527 *Southport* as it roars over Shap summit with a mixed goods heading north, on September 1 1964. Fowler's parallel-boilered 'Baby Scots' were introduced in 1930 - many were rebuilt by Stanier from 1946 with taper boilers. No. 45527 was withdrawn in the week of December 5 1964 from Carlisle Kingmoor after more than 30 years' service.

Right: Grayrigg, September 16 1966: Fairburn 2-6-4T No. 42251 and an unidentified Stanier 'Black Five' blast up the bank with a down freight made up of 'presflow' wagons. The grubby pair of LMS locomotives look work-worn, but are still going strong. Withdrawn in 1967, No. 42251 had one year in service when this photograph was taken. It would eventually find its way to Draper's of Hull, and had been cut up by mid-April 1968.

Left: Power to the North... Gresley 'A3' 4-6-2 No. 60106 *Flying Fox*, complete with German-style smoke deflectors, climbs out of King's Cross with a Gresley Society Special, the 'London North Eastern Flyer', to Doncaster on May 2 1964. Classmate No. 4472 *Flying Scotsman* took over the train at Doncaster for the run to Darlington and back, before No. 60106 took charge again at Doncaster. *Flying Fox* lasted until December 1964 when it was withdrawn from New England shed, Peterborough.

Above: Depots have always been a place for creative photography, where you can get close to the subject for that different angle. The accumulation of oil, grease and dirt on the motion and wheels of an unidentified Stanier 'Black Five' 4-6-0 caught the photographer's eye at Cricklewood on July 24 1965. Low light and an engine in the right position led to this moody photograph - steam in close-up.

Above: The Isle of Wight was, and still is, a haven for vintage locomotives and coaches. Adams, well-known for his radial 4-4-2Ts, also designed the 'O2' 0-4-4Ts such as No. 33 *Bembridge*, departing from Askey on the Isle of Wight in spectacular fashion. The air-braked 48.4-ton, wearing British Railways lined black with the later crest, locomotive had charge of the 14.18pm Ryde to Cowes train on April 6 1965. *Bembridge* stayed on the Isle of Wight until the end of its career and was withdrawn on July 1 1967. The Island still plays host to one member of the class, No. W24 *Calbourne,* based on the Isle of Wight Steam Railway.

Right: Euston before its total destruction in the modernisation of the 1960s: rebuilt 'Patriot' 4-6-0 No. 45530 *Sir Frank Ree* sets out from the LNWR's great London terminus on July 7 1962. The steam from the safety valves betrays that the fireman has built up his fire, in preparation for the slog up Camden bank that lies just ahead.

Above: A grubby 'N' 2-6-0 No. 31856 climbs the bank into Exeter Central from Exeter St Davids with a short two coach train on July 14 1964. The steep grade of the line between the two stations can clearly be seen. At the time No. 31856 was allocated to Exmouth Junction and remained there until withdrawal later that year.

Left: LNWR 'Super D' No. 48930 negotiates Ledburn Crossing, approaching the junction with
the West Coast Main Line at Leighton Buzzard with 'The Banburian' railtour. 'The Banburian' ran from Luton Bute Road to Banbury Merton Street on September 22 1962 with the characteristic '7F' 0-8-0 in charge, for the South Bedfordshire Locomotive Club. No. 48930 was withdrawn on December 4 1962, less than three months after the railtour.

Above: A reminder of past glories - and a foretaste of what is to come. GWR 'Castle' 4-6-0 No. 4079 *Pendennis Castle* is currently under overhaul at Didcot Railway Centre after its return from exile in Australia. But on April 25 1964 even its Antipodean adventures were in the future as it roared through Westbourne Park, West London, with a Festiniog Railway Special. The 1924-built locomotive was bought for preservation direct from BR and ran in the UK before export 'down under' in 1977.

Above: Fowler 2-6-4T No. 42414, allocated to Tebay, climbs Shap with a short freight on July 11 1963. The 2-6-4Ts were introduced in 1927 and 125 were built. Numbered from 42300-42424, Nos. 42398 to 42424 were fitted with side window cabs. No. 42414 was withdrawn in 1964 from Tebay and was later cut up by Hughes Bolckow of Blyth. None survive.

Bottom Left Opposite: Commuting to the capital... Fairburn 2-6-4T No. 42092 races past a Bakerloo line train at Dollis Hill in 1962, heading for Marylebone. The Cricklewood based Fairburn tank still had another two years to go, not being withdrawn until 1964. 40 years on steam still occasionally runs to Marylebone, but the only two surviving 'Fairburns' (Nos. 42073 and 42085) are firmly based at the Lakeside and Haverthwaite Railway.

Above: Strange stablemates... Gresley 'A3' 4-6-2 No. 4472 *Flying Scotsman* and Bulleid 'West Country' No. 34007 *Wadebridge* stand side by side at Nine Elms on May 29 1965. Whilst *Wadebridge* looks distinctly unkempt, for No. 4472 the 'new era' has already begun (it had been bought by Alan Pegler two years earlier). *Wadebridge* was also eventually saved - it left Barry scrapyard in 1981 and although it hasn't yet steamed, restoration is well under way at the Bodmin and Wenford Railway. Could a similar scene one day be repeated?

Above: A favourite location: Vauxhall. In October 1966 one of the distinctive Bulleid 'Light Pacifics', No. 34057 *Biggin Hill*, has charge of a Bournemouth express. Someone has evidently taken the trouble to smarten up the 'Battle of Britain' 4-6-2 - with white-painted buffers, smokebox door handle and lamp irons. *Biggin Hill* ended its working days at Salisbury and was withdrawn on May 7 1967.

Left: With Salisbury Cathedral in the background, Bulleid 'Merchant Navy' No. 35014 *Nederland Line* forges ahead with the down 'Atlantic Coast Express' made up of Bulleid coach set No. 845 on August 3 1964. The end of Southern steam was still almost three years away, and the 'Pacific' lasted until March 1967 - four months before the end. The condition of the lineside is also worthy of note, with neatly ballasted track and an unfenced garden backing on to the line - a scene now changed but still recognisable.

Frank Cassell

■ What started your interest in railways?
I first became interested in railways through my father, who was
a signalman. On leaving school, I went to work
for the railway and stayed until I retired just last year.

■ How did you become interested in railway photography?
I began taking pictures in 1958 and I've done it ever since.
I started out with a box camera and progressed from there. I now use an
Olympus OM40 although in steam days I mostly used a Kodak Sterling.

■ Where were you mainly active?
I went all over the country apart from the Southern Region, but there was
no one regular place that I went to.

■ What was your favourite spot?
I have always liked Devon and Cornwall, as can be seen from some of my
photographs. I particularly liked Torbay and still visit the area today.

■ What was your approach to photography?
I enjoyed taking photographs both by the lineside and in the stations. I
remember one time we stayed in a camping coach
on Hest Back. I could see the trains there 24 hours a day and Alberta a
'Jubilee' which was popular at the time came past on a parcels train. It
was an ideal location and I didn't miss anything!

■ What was your favourite locomotive class?
My favourites were definitely the 'Castles' particularly the single chimney
version.

■ When did your Glorious Years come to an end?
They haven't! I still follow preserved steam and I visit various railways
around the country as well as some of the main line action.

Left: The times they are a-changin': An Albion Super Six passes under a Leicester bridge while 'Standard
5' No. 73040 pauses above. This is July 1 1965 and despite the late date, the Nuneaton-allocated
No. 73040 still has three years to serve. Soon after the picture was taken, No. 73040 moved to Croes
Newydd, and was withdrawn on May 11 1968 from Patricroft, a name associated so closely with the
end of steam.

Above: GWR 'Hall' No. 6931 *Aldborough Hall* works hard as it climbs away from Par in Cornwall with a mixture of vehicles, including two road milk tanks. This is May 3 1960, when No. 6931 was allocated to Taunton. However, two months later it exchanged the West Country for the West Midlands, when it moved to Wolverhampton Stafford Road in the week of July 30. *Aldborough Hall* lasted almost until the end of Western steam, being withdrawn from Oxford on September 25 1965.

Above: Push-pull fitted Fowler 2-6-2T No. 40010 makes a lively departure from Leicester with the 4.10pm Leicester-Nuneaton train on May 24 1960. With its four LMS coaches, the '3P' is a reminder of local trains in the 1960s and before - an era by now already being cast aside with the DMU revolution. Allocated to Nuneaton, No. 40010 would move twice in a career destined to last just over another year: to Stafford at the end of the year, and then Willesden, from where it was withdrawn on July 20 1961. The class of 70 2-6-2Ts were - reportedly - poor performers. Twenty were fitted with condensing equipment for use on London suburban trains into Moorgate.

Above: Vintage beauty as Beattie well tank No. 30586 shunts at Wadebridge on May 3 1960. By then, this engine and Nos. 30585 and 30587 were minor celebrities - the final survivors of a class dating back to 1863. The trio were retained especially for working the Wenfordbridge branch. Sadly, this was the only one of the three not to survive. It was withdrawn from Wadebridge on December 29 1962.

Above: 'Royal Scot' No. 46154 *The Hussar* stands at a grimy Manchester Central on May 22 1959. It is in final form, rebuilt with tapered boiler and curved smoke deflectors, which make it look very different from its original parallel-boilered appearance. No. 46154 was London-based, transferred to Kentish Town just two weeks before this picture was taken. The 4-6-0 moved a lot in its life, being transferred no fewer than 20 times between 1930 and withdrawal (from Willesden) in June 1963.

Above: The GWR lives... More than 12 years after Nationalisation, 'Castle' No. 5020 *Trematon Castle* storms away from Par with a Manchester to Penzance 'inter-regional' on May 5 1960. No. 5020 - lacking a shedcode plate - was a Taunton engine, but would move to Exeter just a month later.
The 'Castle' was withdrawn in the week of November 10 1962 from Llanelly.

Bottom Left Opposite: Shafts of sunlight pour through the roof onto polished GWR 4-6-0 No. 1020 *County of Monmouth* at Neyland shed on May 8 1961. Allocated to Neyland since 1956, the Hawksworth 'County' had three years to go until withdrawal from Swindon on February 26 1964. Introduced in 1945, 30 'Counties' were built but all were cut up. Tentative plans to 'recreate' one using a 'Modified Hall' and '8F' boiler from the 'Barry Ten' have been mooted (SR268).

Above: There are some things that preservation can never recreate! This is Syston Junction on July 22 1960, with 'Jubilee' No. 45565 *Victoria* haring along with the noon Bradford-St Pancras. Speeding the other way, on the left, is rebuilt 'Patriot' No. 45532 *Illustrious,* with the 12.55pm St Pancras-Nottingham, and on the right is the former Crosti '9F' No. 92025, held at signals with a Clay Cross to Ashwell freight. Happy days...

Right: The Western Region at its best as the chocolate and cream Mk 1s of the 'Cornishman' roll into Par behind 'County' No. 1008 *County of Cardigan.* If your carriage pulled up alongside the station nameboard, it certainly would be difficult to mistake where you were. The Carlyon Bay hotel, in Newquay, was once company-owned, hence the rather large billing! No. 1008's last allocation was, Swindon from where it was withdrawn on October 3 1963.

Above: Gresley 'K3/2' No. 61966 races through Quorn with an up fish train on May 24 1960. Such fast freight duties were typical for the 'K3s', built between 1920 and 1937. The location is well known and still sees steam today - it is now part of Leicestershire's Great Central Railway. The LNER 'Mogul' was at the time allocated to Immingham. It remained there until July 9 1961 when it was transferred to Colwick. All 'K3s' were withdrawn by 1962, the end for No. 61966 coming in February.

Left: Shades of The Titfield Thunderbolt: Collett 'auto-tank' No. 1419 waits at Fowey on May 3 1960 with the 5.35pm to Losthwithiel, where the Fowey branch connected with the main line. On the left are china clay wagons, the lifeline of the branch. This traffic still uses the branch today although the modern wagons bear little resemblance to these and the station is long gone. No. 1419 was withdrawn on April 27 1961 from St Blazey, its home since December 1949.

Above: St Blazey's surviving half-roundhouse was recently in the news when it was put up for sale for £60,000 (SR259). But on May 11 1960 it was busy with GWR locomotives - many for the local china clay traffic. Collett 0-6-0PT No. 3635 takes centre-stage on the turntable, while the later Hawksworth-designed '16XX' No. 1664 rests in the background on the left. In addition to another pannier, 'Small Prairie' No. 5539 is to left.

Above: The crew of LMS 4-6-0 No. 46112 *Sherwood Forester* are certainly aware of the cameraman at Syston East Junction on April 10 1961. The immaculate rebuilt 'Royal Scot' - a credit to Nottingham shed - is working from Queniborough to Leicester with empty stock, ready to take a football special on to Swindon. The 4-6-0 did not survive, being withdrawn in May 1964 from Annesley, but Nos. 46100 and 46115 did, and there are hopes that No. 46115 might return to the main line (SR268/269).

Above: A peaceful, rural scene, and a big, grimy freight engine... 'WD' 2-8-0 No. 90438 on a typical working
for the class - heavy freight - passes the signalbox and former station at Rearsby on August 14 1962. The architecture of Rearsby, on the line from Syston Junction to Melton Mowbray, clearly shows its
Midland Railway ancestry. The Riddles locomotive is just one of 935 'Austerity' 2-8-0s - branded by some as "cheap and nasty '8Fs'" - built for the Army. At this time No. 90438 was allocated to Colwick.
It was withdrawn from there on October 3 1965 and scrapped at Draper's of Hull.

Above: You can almost smell the smoke, from countless household chimneys as well as '8F' 2-8-0 No. 48268, as the 1942-built Stanier 2-8-0 romps through Tiviot Dale, Stockport, with a short eastbound freight on December 28 1963. No. 48268 was at this time a Warrington engine. Withdrawal came in the week ending October 28 1967 from Edge Hill. This picture embodies the railway in the North West - gritty, grimy, but full of character and atmosphere. Glorious years indeed!

David Forsyth

■ **What started your railway interest?**

The family home was in Cheadle Hulme and during wartime we used to go to Brough - Westmorland for an autumn break - I would have been six or seven. My father took me over to Penrith during the early afternoons to see the constant stream of streamliners and original 'Scots' pounding up to Shap. I was hooked and still am: I still take pictures of the West Coast Main Line today from the same place.

■ **How did you become interested in photography?**

Photography was a natural follow-on from my interest in trains. I was inspired by the published work of Eric Treacy - and later by E.D. Broome - and set out to emulate them at the age of about 12. I failed, of course! I was using a borrowed camera which made getting reasonable shots of moving trains out of the question. But then I joined the RCTS and was influenced by its policy of photographing the last examples of classes, and to make the locomotives themselves the subjects of my shots. That was in 1957. In steam days I always took black and white: when I was at university, it was a question of cost (I economised on food to pay for film), but even later on I stuck to it, mainly because the light was often so bad and the engines so dirty!

■ **Do you have any regrets?**

Steam-wise it has to be that I wasn't competent earlier, so I missed a lot of the older types. But ironically I now also regret that I didn't bother to photograph the early years of the DMUs, which were such a part of that transition era. Nevertheless, I would do it all over again in a similar way, without question.

■ **Where were your preferred photographic spots?**

I always took photographs in the local area, as it's always been my philosophy to record the changing scene. For me that meant two places - the GNR(I) Belfast-Dublin main line in Northern Ireland, where I was teaching between 1961 and 1966, and Carlisle, where my parents lived and where I spent eight weeks every summer during those crucial last years of steam. I was lucky with Carlisle in that it was a tremendous steam centre even late-on. I tried to get pictures of all locomotives allocated to Carlisle - though of course I never did! Things were a little more thin on the ground in Northern Ireland but there were tremendous sights - blue 4-4-0s on coaches dating from the turn of the century, for instance.

■ **When did your glorious years come to an end?**

There was a pause from April 1968 when I got married and moved to Kenilworth in Warwickshire, where steam had already disappeared. After a while I took up modern traction photography in a haphazard manner, but after the 'return to steam', main line steam once again became my absolute priority. That changed in the mid-1980s, when, with the working railway changing so quickly - I decided to broaden my horizons. I now mostly record the changing WCML scene.

Left: The atmosphere of steam on damp, rainy days was wonderful, if admittedly tricky to photograph. On Saturday August 13 1966, filthy BR '5MT' No. 73128, lacking a smokebox numberplate but having retained its Patricroft shedplate, did not seem a promising choice to take over at Carlisle from 'Britannia' No. 70005 *John Milton* on the 2pm Glasgow-Liverpool. I learnt subsequently that the 4-6-0 had to be taken off with brake trouble at Preston, where there was an hour's delay before 'Black Five' No. 45197 could be substituted.

Above: When I was teaching at a school in Northern Ireland from 1961-66, the Ulster Transport Authority's ex-GNR(I) line around Belfast became a regular haunt. Even in the mid-1960s pre-Grouping style scenes could still be seen, such as this of ex-GNR(I) 'SG' 0-6-0 No. 44 plugging through Lisburn with a long afternoon mixed goods from Portadown to Belfast on February 29 1964.

Right: How many people's fascination with steam started at the platform end? Kingmoor's 'Coronation' No. 46257 *City of Salford* is the subject of spotters' attention at Carlisle as it waits to take the 11.30am Birminghan New Street-Edinburgh (Princes Street) train forward on August 14 1964. It had taken over here from English Electric Type No. 4 D211 *Mauretania*. This was to be my last encounter with an LMS-designed 'Pacific' in revenue-earning service.

Right: 'Duchesses' were still to be seen in the summer of 1964, and on August 11 No. 46237 *City of Bristol* has just reversed a parcels train from Crewe into one of the lines allocated to parcels traffic opposite Carlisle's Platform 1. Alongside the 'Coronation' is another 'Pacific', Kingmoor's No. 70007 *Coeur de Lion*, which will take out a parcels train later in the afternoon. No. 70007 was the first 'Britannia' to be withdrawn, in June 1965. No. 46237 went just a month after this picture was taken, in the week ending September 12 1964.

Above: Queuing to join the main line at Carlisle's Upperby Bridge Junction... On July 2 1966 'Black Five' No. 45376 is waiting to go on to Upperby shed, but must wait its turn for a path - stuck behind a freight. A second goods waits its turn after the LMS 4-6-0, hauled by single-chimney '9F' No. 92012, itself a resident of Carlisle Kingmoor.

Left: The summer of 1963 was the last in which 'Royal Scots' could be seen in quantity on the West Coast Main Line (the first 'Scots' - Nos. 46100 and 46139 - were withdrawn in October 1962, the last - No. 46115 - in January 1966). Here No. 46115 *Scots Guardsman* (a Longsight locomotive and now preserved) is watered before leaving Upperby shed on July 13 1963 to haul train the 8am Aberdeen-Manchester Victoria, while Crewe North's No. 46165 *The Ranger (12th London Regiment)* simmers behind. On the left is an unidentified 'Black Five' and in the distance several other engines can also be seen.

Above: Rationalisation has clearly manifested itself in the lifted lines on the right as Stanier '5MT' 4-6-0 No. 44790 blasts smokily out of Carlisle on July 2 1966. On summer Saturdays that year there were still 14 steam-hauled passenger trains over Shap, including this one, the 1.25pm Glasgow Central to Morecambe (Promenade). In the background, the cavern-like Carlisle train-shed looms above the exhausts of other locomotives, dominating the cityscape.

Right: On February 29 1964 ex-GNR(I) 'VS' 4-4-0 No. 207 *Boyne* waits at Adelaide MPD. The next day it would head a Sunday Belfast to Dublin excursion, its only regular duty. *Boyne* was bought by the UTA from the Irish Republic's CIE in 1963. Its original nameplates were removed before the sale, and replaced by wooden ones. The 4-4-0 retained its GNR number and blue livery until withdrawal in 1965.

Above: Carlisle again and in a scene typical of the last years of steam, 'Black Five' No. 45295 leaves the city (with the station visible in the background) at the head of the 9.50am Saturdays-only from Edinburgh (Waverley)-Leeds on July 17 1965. Although it's in typically filthy condition, someone has given the Kingmoor 4-6-0's cabside number a wipe-over to keep its identity legible.

Left: The station building at Cumwhinton (closed on November 5 1956) has been taken over by a tyre company as 'Jubilee' No. 45742 *Connaught* runs through with the featherweight 4.37pm Carlisle-Bradford (Forster Square) on June 30 1964. The grimy *Connaught*, a Kingmoor engine, was withdrawn in September 1964.

Above: 'Across the water' in Northern Ireland, 'Jeep' 2-6-4T No. 53 clearly shows its Derby ancestry as the LMS (Northern Counties Committee) engine starts crisply from Lisburn with the Saturdays-only 1.45pm Belfast (Great Victoria Street)-Portadown on November 9 1963.

Right Below Opposite: A shed scene that evokes long, hot summers as engines simmer at Adelaide, Northern Ireland, on September 14 1963. Dominating the picture is ex-LMS(NCC) 'W' 2-6-0 No. 94 *The Maine*. Creeping in on the right is the former GNR(I) 'SG3' 0-6-0 No. 34, while behind the 'Mogul', GNR(I) 'S' 4-4-0 No. 60 *Slieve Donard* is having its smokebox emptied. Behind the 4-4-0, smoke drifts lazily from the chimney of GNR(I) 'SG' 0-6-0 No. 44.

Above: Powering south past semaphores near Leyland on the West Coast Main Line is single-chimney '9F' No. 92016 on September 5 1964. It is a classic railway scene – but in the background the modern road shows very clearly the shape of things to come. The 2-10-0 was still just ten years old, being new to Wellingborough on October 7 1954. But despite being designed for 40 years' work, the Riddles engine lasted just another three – giving it a total lifespan of 13 years. It was withdrawn in the week of October 21 1967 and was cut up by Motherwell Machinery and Scrap of Wishaw after being sent from Carnforth LNW on January 18 1968.

Ray Farrell

■ What started your interest?

I think it was when I was about ten or 11 and I remember taking numbers down locally. It was an interest that grew over the years as I discovered the West Coast Main Line, from being at school at Bolton near Wigan. The interest waned to an extent when I left to school, but things changed again in 1958 when my interest in railway photography was sparked off.

■ How did you become interested in railway photography?

I saw a picture by Bishop Eric Treacy on the cover of Trains Illustrated which rekindled my interest in photography and trains. It was a picture of a 'Royal Scot' and I read the magazine cover to cover three or four times over.

■ What was your favourite spot?

My favourite line was the West Coast Main Line because of the glamour associated with the named trains such as the 'Caledonian' and the 'Mid-Day Scot'. There was also a huge volume of steam power on the WCML in the 1958-68 period. I enjoyed visiting Leeds to see the Eastern Region locomotives as it was something a bit different and I also had a lineside permit for these areas.

■ What was your approach to photography?

'Conventional' would be the best way to describe it! I started in 1958 locally around the Bury, Bolton and Wigan areas. I was interested in locomotives rather than the infrastructure and would rather have seen an engine with a good exhaust than standing in a station.

I had a lineside pass for sections of the London Midland and Eastern Regions and so often took pictures well away from the stations.

Water troughs held a great fascination for me as well as the glamour of the West Coast Main line, where I spent many hours, between Wigan and Preston.

■ When did your Glorious Years come to an end?

August 3 1968! This was a sad and sudden occasion for me, as I never thought I would see the day when there were no working steam locomotives owned by BR. With preservation unfolding new opportunities, my interest was rekindled, especially with the East Lancashire Railway on my doorstep. Preservation also made the 'impossible' possible. Sights such as 'A4' No. 60007 Sir Nigel Gresley and 'A3' No. 4472 Flying Scotsman on the ELR, for example. Something that would never have happened in BR days!

Above: With LMS coaches in tow and smoking tank engines on the right, this could almost be a pre-Nationalisation scene as 'Jubilee' No. 45565 *Victoria* departs from Leeds City. However, the picture dates from August 8 1959. On the immediate right is an Ivatt '2MT' 2-6-2T and further back a 2-6-4T. On the left, a line of horseboxes awaits new work. At the time of this picture No. 45565 was allocated to Holbeck, remaining there until June 1962. Leeds City is currently the subject of a major renovation scheme to improve passenger facilities and increase capacity at this important Yorkshire interchange.

Right: Double-chimney 'A3' 4-6-2 No. 60044 *Melton* rounds the curve north of York station with a train for Newcastle on August 10 1962. Note the impressive permanent way, and the well-kept shrubs. The Gresley 'Pacific' displays the final condition of the class but is still - for now - on 'top link' duties.

Above: World steam speed record holder *Mallard* slides into King's Cross with an express from the North. The 'A4', which famously achieved 126mph in 1938, by now wears BR's Brunswick Green and the number 60022 - as well as having lost its side valances. This is March 1962 and *Mallard* is about to enter its final year in service. The 4-6-2 was withdrawn on April 25 1963 from 'Top Shed' after being allocated there for fully 15 years. Fortunately, it was saved for the nation and is now, restored to original condition, on display at the National Railway Museum.

Left: The last gasp of the steam age as Stanier '8F' No. 48338 climbs Miles Platting bank out of Manchester in spectacular style on May 15 1968. The Stanier 2-8-0 was in its last month of service, being withdrawn in the week of June 8 1968. Signs of the period of this photograph include the painted depot code on the smokebox door and the new yellow ends of the DMU lurking to the right. The mixed freight train includes a BR Mk 1 BG parcels van directly behind the locomotive.

Above: The crew holds a discussion as they fill the water tanks of Fowler 'Jinty' No. 47584 on Bury Loop next to Bury East signalbox on December 4 1959. Allocated to Bury the '3F' moved in February 1964 to Patricroft, from where it was withdrawn in the week of July 18 1964. The class of 412 locomotives, introduced in 1924 by the LMS, were often to be found on local freight and passenger trains and also as station and goods pilots. Ten are preserved including one, No. 47324, based near this location at the East Lancashire Railway.

Right: 'K3' No. 61940 heads a local passenger train away from Leeds Central on June 25 1960. Allocated to March from January 1948, the Gresley 2-6-0 moved to Doncaster on September 16 1956 and remained there until withdrawal on May 4 1962. Like the 'K3', Leeds Central is now long gone - it was decided in 1963 to concentrate all services on Leeds City station. However, some signs that Leeds Central existed can still be found. The nearby ex-North Eastern Railway roundhouse survives, as does the viaduct across the River Aire.

Above: Steam seems to ooze from every pore of '4F' No. 44489 as it heads an eastbound freight through Castleton, near Manchester. It is a crisp and wintry November 7 1964. The 0-6-0 was allocated to Trafford Park and survived for just one more year before withdrawal, from Workington in the week of August 28 1965. No. 44489 was sold to Birds Commercial Motors where it was sent on November 15 1965 along with Nos. 44449, 44536 and 48774, for cutting up.

Left: Departing northbound from Leeds Central via the short spur for connecting with the lines from Leeds City is BR '4MT' 2-6-4T No. 80118 with a local passenger working on June 25 1960. The locomotive carries the larger Scottish Region-style numbers on the side of the bunker. It was allocated to Neville Hill at the time but moved north in October 1963, initially being loaned to Carstairs and then allocated there from November 3 1963. No. 80118 was withdrawn on November 29 1966 and was sold to Motherwell Machinery and Scrap at Wishaw. Of 155 built, 15 of the class survive in preservation.

Above: Rebuilt 'Patriot' No. 45545 Planet, in clean condition for the period, tops the climb from Wigan to Boars Head with a northbound freight on October 5 1963. Initially allocated to Kentish Town when new in March 1934, the 4-6-0 only stayed there for three months. From February 1935, No. 45545 was based at various WCML depots including Crewe South, Longsight, Willesden, Camden and Edge Hill. At the time of the photograph, No. 45545 was allocated to Upperby and it was withdrawn from there in the week of May 30 1964.

Above: The up 'Caledonian' speeds along the WCML between Madeley and Whitmore troughs south of Crewe. It is September 4 1959 and Camden's 'Princess Coronation' No. 46245 City of London is in charge. Appropriately, given its name, No. 46245 was a London engine for almost its entire life. It was allocated to Camden from new in June 1943, and only moved to Willesden (on the closure of Camden) in the week of September 7 1963. Its last days were spent at Crewe North, from where it was withdrawn in the week of July 18 1964.

Left: Gresley 'A3' No. 60107 Royal Lancer makes a rousing departure from Leeds Central as it heads south along the East Coast Main Line to King's Cross on April 24 1963. The 'Pacific' - in final condition with double chimney and German-style smoke deflectors - was by this time allocated to Grantham, from where it was withdrawn on September 1 1963. Neither locomotive nor location still exist, No. 60107 was cut up at Doncaster Works before the year was out and Leeds trains now all use Leeds City.

Left: Plenty of fodder for the spotters at York Roundhouse on May 21 1966 with 'K1' 2-6-0 No. 62065, 'V2' 2-6-2 No. 60806, 'Black Five' No. 45339 and Ivatt '4MT' 2-6-0 No. 43133 awaiting their next duties. Of the four locomotives, only No. 45339 was a visitor, being allocated to Rose Grove. Sadly none survived into preservation. The first to be withdrawn was No. 60806 in September 1966 (from York North), then No. 43133 in December 1966 (from North Blyth); third was the 'K1' (from York North) in March 1967, and finally the 'Black Five' ended its working days at Lostock Hall, in July 1967.

Peter Fitton

■ What started your interest in railways?

I was born in Doncaster but we moved to a house overlooking the Fylde Coast line at St Annes in 1949, when I was six. I clearly remember seeing *Windward Isles* - the 'Jubilee' destroyed at Harrow, running into Blackpool in about 1951.

■ How did you become interested in photography?

I started taking pictures in 1958, influenced by local photographer Frank Dean. My first efforts weren't very good, but I persevered and in 1959 bought a Retinette 35mm camera. Colour (either Kodachrome or Ektachrome) followed in 1961, but the amount I took depended on finances. In 1963 I changed cameras, buying a Pentax S1A for £90 - which meant I couldn't afford colour for a while afterwards! I have around 10,000 negatives from steam days and a couple of thousand slides, plus what I've taken subsequently.

■ Where were your favourite 'haunts'?

There was so much going on around Blackpool in those days that I mostly stuck to the local area, although I did utilise holidays to see other parts of the country as well. We cycled to spots that were very close, and used the 'Runabout' tickets to get a bit further afield. In 1962, I spent six months at Rugby, where I took a lot more pictures. Then from 1964-67 I attended university in Bradford, so most pictures from that period were taken around there.

■ Do you have any regrets?

Not really, although it's true to say that I did my fair share of trying to catch things before it was too late - and frequently missed! Although I was never a member of the MNA, I was a sort of 'honorary' member. We used to clean engines at Blackpool and Low Moor - I was brought up on 'Jubilees', and *Victoria* (No. 45565) was a particular favourite. One regret, though, is that I never saw all the 'Jubes' - No. 45711 *Courageous* always eluded me.

■ What did you do after the end of steam?

I carried on with modern traction photography, but aside from trips to the Keighley and Worth Valley Railway, didn't follow the preserved scene much until the 'Return to Steam' in 1971. I had always been interested in the main line - and I still am. Also, as time went on, I travelled abroad increasingly, to places like Pakistan and China. But I still take pictures in the local area - 40 years on, steam still comes to Blackpool occasionally - and I sometimes visit the West Highland Line for the 'Jacobites'. I am also involved with *Duchess of Sutherland* - as a patron of the Princess Royal Class Locomotive Trust. Let's face it, the 'Coronations' are the finest engines ever built!

Left: Before such pictures became 'hackneyed', Fairburn '4MT' No. 42073 simmers in Low Moor shed yard on December 14 1966. A brazier burning to keep the water column from freezing illuminates the 2-6-4T's front end, while yard lights pick out indistinct shapes of engines in the background. The re-creation of a similar scene is not impossible - Low Moor has gone, but No. 42073 in action at the Lakeside and Haverthwaite Railway.

Above: Shap was a magnet for enthusiasts in the North West - and with such scenes it's no wonder. At Grayrigg on July 12 1964, '4MT' No. 42449 pilots rebuilt 'Patriot' No. 45512 Bunsen towards the summit with a Manchester to Glasgow train. The Shap pilot and banking engines were at this point being provided by Carnforth following the closure of Oxenholme shed in June 1962. From June 1965, they came - except on Sundays - from Tebay.

Above: Steam over Shap has just another 11 days to go as '8F' No. 48491 blasts unaided towards the summit at Scout Green with a non-fitted goods train on December 20 1967. This shot, of a grimy, leaky engine working hard through the snow-speckled hills, is typical of steam's last winter.

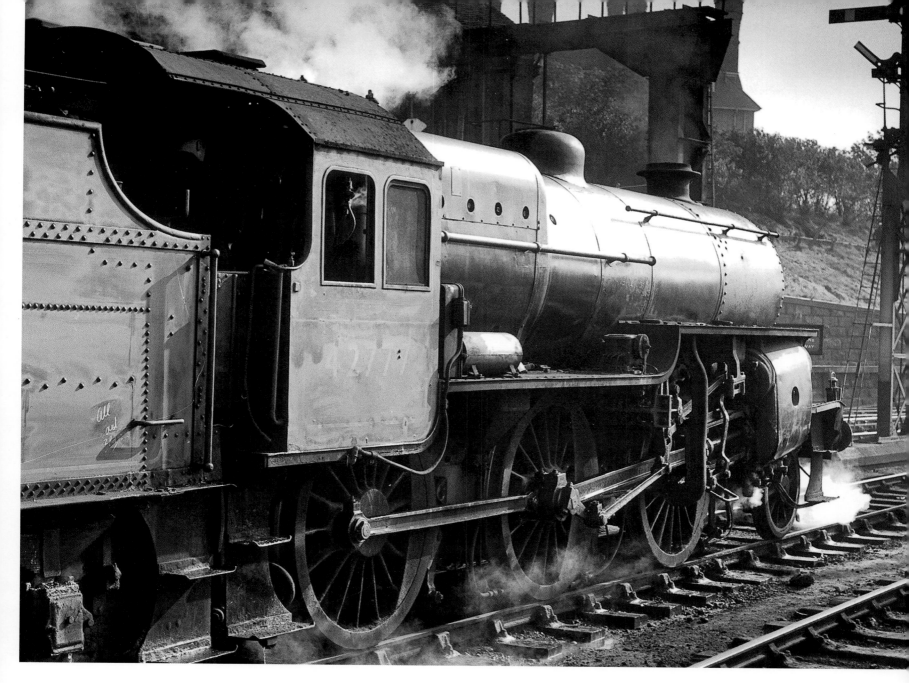

Above: LMS 'Crab' No. 42777 'catches the glint' at Preston south bay in the early afternoon of October 12 1963. The 'dolly' is off to allow the 2-6-0 to move out of the bay, ready to take a train on to Manchester. The 'Crab' still has another couple of years before being withdrawn, which took place in the week ending August 14 1965.

Above: Until 1967 there was still a tremendous variety of steam to be seen including - before steam in the North East ended on September 9 - scenes such as this. On August 31, 'J27' No. 65882 heads into the evening sun on the Silksworth branch. Despite the late date, the chunky 0-6-0 is in good external condition - due to efforts of the local enthusiasts.

Left: An overcast day does nothing to dampen the excitement of the platform end, as seen in the faces of the 'locospotters' on the right. Steam roars from the safety valves of 'Royal Scot' No. 46160 Queen Victoria's Rifleman at Leeds City on November 2 1959. With the headboard already in place, the Fowler/Stanier 4-6-0 is waiting to work the up 'Thames-Clyde Express' to St Pancras, before returning to its home shed of Kentish Town. This became the last engine we ever cleaned at Blackpool Central shed, in September 1964.

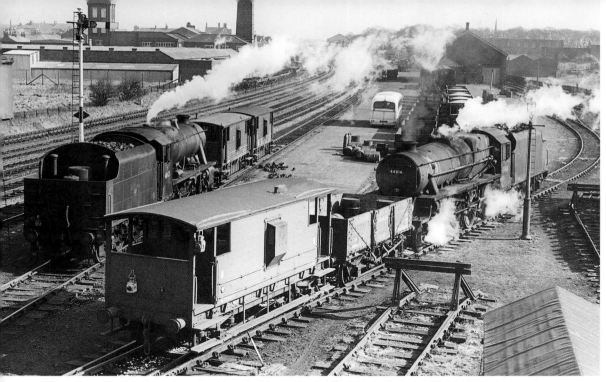

Above: I've called this picture 'lunch break' and that is exactly what it is. This is the former LYR and LNWR Joint goods yard at Kirkham, on March 7 1968. Stanier '8F' No. 48423 and 'Black Five' No. 44816, two of BR's few remaining steam locomotives, simmer in the sun. The 2-8-0 is on a local trip freight, and the 4-6-0 on a permanent way working. It looks timeless, but before the end of the summer such scenes would be gone forever.

Above: Backlighting catches the side of Gresley 'V2' No. 60877 as it leaves York with a northbound parcels train on the morning of October 24 1964. This was exactly the work the 'V2s' - a mixed traffic design - were built for. No. 60877, built as No. 4848 in June 1940, served the LNER and BR for 26 years, before being withdrawn on February 13 1966.

Bottom Left Opposite: A penny for the thoughts of the crew of 2-6-4T No. 42174 as it simmers in Manchester Victoria's Platform 13 on April 21 1965, having arrived with the 8am from Orrell. No. 42174, one of the Fairburn series of '4MTs', represented the final phase of an LMS family of locomotives which stretched back to the parallel-boilered Fowler version of 1927. Two 'Fairburns' survive - Nos. 42073 and 42085 are both on the Lakeside and Haverthwaite Railway.

Above: A flashback to the last year of the 'Kings', as No. 6015 King Richard III runs into Banbury from the north with the 6.30am Birkenhead-Paddington train on July 20 1962. On the right, the driver of Woodford Halse 'B1' 4-6-0 No. 61116 looks back at the camera as he waits for the road.

Above: Plenty of evening mood, but there's nothing here to suggest this is the final week before closure of this station. Riddles '2MT' 2-6-2T No. 84025 waits at Horwich with a push-pull train to Chorley alongside Stanier two-cylinder '4MT' 2-6-4T No. 42484, with the 4.54pm to Bolton. It is September 20 1965 - Horwich station closed to passengers on September 27.

Above: The yellow cabside stripe dates this picture as a later steam view, denoting that 'Jubilee' No. 45721 *Impregnable* is not allowed to run under the wires south of Crewe. *Impregnable*, pictured on September 1 1965, is standing in the part of the station demolished in 1974. The Stanier 4-6-0's presentable condition is not a coincidence - it had been 'unofficially' cleaned by myself and Paul Claxton, a friend and MNA member.

Above: An unidentified 0-6-0PT, lacking a smokebox numberplate, trundles through Llangollen station with an afternoon freight from Bala to Ruabon in July 1954. It is Eisteddfod time and the bunting is out in Abbey Road. On the right, an old Crosville 'N' Class Leyland Cub bus has been tarted up and transformed into a mobile booking office, and a Morris Oxford lurks at the bottom of the slope. Happily, the scene has changed very little - today the station is the headquarters of the Llangollen Railway.

Left: The 'Standard four' may be a BR locomotive, but apart from that this scene is pure pre-Nationalisation. On April 3 1965, 4-6-0 No. 75017 pauses at Gargrave's wooden platform with the 12.22pm Skipton-Morecambe, formed of two ex-LMS vehicles. By now based at Skipton, the '4MT' was withdrawn from there in the week ending January 7 1967.

Bill Rear

■ **How did you become interested in photography?**
My family always had an interest in photography, but usually only family snaps. They had a holiday cottage at Betws Garmon near Caernarfon and a couple of the earliest snaps were of the Welsh Highland Railway. I started photography myself when I was about 12. I concentrated on railways in the landscape - I felt there were already enough three-quarter front views of engines and trains.

■ **What was your first camera?**
The inevitable 120 size Box Brownie that was given as a cast-off present! I graduated to a 120 Wirgin camera with three shutter speeds and an f6.3 lens before I was 'taken in hand' by a professional photographer who was the father of childhood friends and tutored on a plate Ensign 'Popular Pressman'. With six single plateholders loaded with glass plates, you learned to be very careful and economical, especially when you had to hump everything around with you. I next acquired an Agfa Isolette before changing to 35mm format. Since then I have fluctuated between 35mm and the larger format which I prefer. Current cameras are a 35mm Canon EOS5 and a Mamiya 645.

■ **What were your favourite locations?**
The Llanberis and Afon Wen branches, although I took photographs wherever I could. A lot were taken around Crewe, where I worked as a fireman until I left BR in 1958.

■ **How did you reach these locations?**
Being a railwayman, I usually scrounged a lift off the Bangor men who worked both the Llanberis and Afon Wen branches. Otherwise I cycled. After passing my driving test in 1951, I borrowed my mother's Morris Minor for more distant trips. Afon Wen, Bangor, Caernarvon and Portmadoc were the most frequently visited spots local to my then home at Waenfawr.

■ **When did your glorious years end?**
After leaving the railway, I joined Crosville Motor Services Ltd (the North Wales bus operator) before going to university as a mature student and becoming a teacher near Wrexham. About 1958 I lost interest in photography generally, only rarely taking the odd railway view. My interest was first resurrected in the 1980s.

Left: A nostalgic rural view of Port Siding signalbox (on the Menai Bridge-Afon Wen line) in May 1950 as Aspinall '3F' 0-6-0 No. 52407 works the Port Siding to Port Dinorwic harbour trip freight. In the middle distance Stanier '4MT' 2-6-4T No. 42460 picks up wagons for Menai Bridge yard while working a Llanberis goods, and something has obviously attracted the attention of the signalmen halfway up the signalbox steps on the left! The little '3F' was withdrawn on January 26 1951 and cut up on April 7 the same year.

Above: LMS '4F' No. 4476 plods northwards from Carnforth on a ballast train at .9pm on August 30 964. I remember a 'Coronation' came roaring through about five minutes later - it must have caught the '4F' up pretty quickly! The coaling plant of Carnforth MPD can be seen in the background (above the tender), and on the right are the remains of the Second World War ordnance depot.

Above: British Railways '4MT' 4-6-0 No. 75012 shunts the well-filled yard at Chester General station one bright morning in February 1952, as the crew pose for the camera. I remember the driver was less than complimentary about his steed - in fact, his comments were somewhat rude!

Above: Memories of summer holidays, at Caernarvon Seiont Sidings in August 1952. Caught in the sun, Stanier '4MT' 2-6-4T No. 42444 leans into the sharp curve near the entrance to the disused brickworks sidings with the daily excursion train - reporting number W635 - from Rhyl to Llanberis.

Above: It is a glorious summer's day in July 1953 as 'Black Five' No. 45385 pulls away from Colwyn Bay station with a Saturdays-only train to Llandudno. Note the varied assortment of coaches in the train, all but one of which are now in BR livery. Today this scene has completely changed – now there are only two tracks and the formation has been moved slightly seawards to accommodate the A55 Expressway which runs on the old trackbed.

Above: An Ivatt 'Mickey Mouse' 2-6-0 approaches the former Welsh Highland Railway crossing near Portmadoc in June 1953 with the afternoon working of the Rhyl 'Landcruise' train. The train is formed of a very mixed bag of stock - the leading coach is one of the 'Coronation Scot' corridor brake third vehicles which went to America in 1939. It was built without a corridor connection at the guard's compartment end. Leaning from the cab is driver Frank Beech of Rhyl shed.

Below Left Opposite: A view of Britannia Bridge from the Caernarvon side in July 1953. Holyhead resident, clean Stanier '5MT' 4-6-0 No. 45110 (now preserved at the Severn Valley Railway) rounds the curve out of the Tubular Bridge. The 'Black Five' is working wrong line, with a Holyhead to Manchester express. Saturday single-line working over the bridge was rare, but I understand that a broken rail had been found in the tunnel earlier in the day.

Right: The last day of passenger services at Ringwood. In the afternoon of May 4 1964, '3MT' No. 82028 makes a spirited departure from Ringwood for Bournemouth with a train for Brockenhurst. A small headboard marks the occasion.

Above: One of Maunsell's chunky 'Qs', No. 30548 of Bournemouth shed, trundles towards Brockenhurst with a morning Ringwood-line pick-up goods. The 0-6-0 has just joined the main line at Lymington Junction. The 'Q' - in its later condition as modified by Bulleid with a Lemaitre large-diameter chimney - was allocated to Bournemouth at Nationalisation, and apart from a month on the books of Stewarts Lane in 1949, remained there until the week of January 5 1963. It then moved to Eastleigh until withdrawn on March 21 1965.

Jim Read

What started your interest in railways?
I think I was a born enthusiast. At the age of only about four or five, I clearly remember seeing a GWR pannier tank heading into Birkenhead with express headlamps on. At around the same time, I apparently asked my father why engines always 'pulled' their steam!

How did you become interested in photography?
I was interested in railways for a long time before I became interested in photography. Even after I bought a camera, I didn't take pictures of steam locomotives for quite a while. It wasn't until 1952 when I moved to Stratford-upon-Avon, and there met the photographer T.E. Williams, that I started to become interested.

Most of your photographs seem to be taken in the New Forest area. Why was that?
I moved to Ringwood, Hampshire, in 1956. At first I was a cinema projectionist, which meant working on Saturdays, and even after I changed jobs the factory I worked in was open most Saturdays, so I had limited time - and no car. Inevitably most of my pictures were taken in the local area. But I'm afraid I was a 'born and bred' GWR and LMS man, and it was quite a while before I could muster much interest in 'Spam Cans'!

What was your favourite spot?
Although many of my photographs were taken on the Ringwood line, where I took many pictures from the road bridge just outside Ringwood station, my all-time favourite was Sway on the main line. It was a lovely open spot and engines worked hard there. After services on the Ringwood line finished in 1964, I concentrated on the main line.

Do you have any regrets?
Mainly that although I concentrated on the local area, there were still many places nearby that I didn't photograph.

Did you follow steam after 1968?
I still live in Ringwood and both the Mid-Hants and Swanage Railways are within striking distance. With better film, a better camera - and more skill - I'm able to take far better pictures than I ever could in steam days!

Why publish your pictures now?
I thought for years that the pictures were of little interest to anyone, and it was only after I retired that I printed many of them for the first time. The negatives taken around Stratford-on-Avon area had been lost, but the Ringwood ones were still intact and I was surprised how many I had! Ironically, I recently sold the Leica (bought for £36, in about 1960) for £150, so it wasn't a bad buy.

Right: Bournemouth-based 'M7' No. 30058 scampers away from Ringwood with a train for Brockenhurst in spring 1960. The take over fitted 0-4-4T carries 'dog' fastenings on the smokebox door in addition to the central 'dart' handle. In the background, a variety of goods stock stands in Ringwood station's small yard.

Left: BR '3MT' 2-6-2T No. 82027 leaves Ringwood with a Bournemouth-Brockenhurst train. Nothing remains of this view today: the yard to the right has been covered by housing, to the left is an industrial estate and the railway itself is a road. Nor did any of the 'Standard 3s' survive. Designed at Swindon in 1952, the boilers were based on those of the GWR 'Large Prairies'. The last two, Nos. 82019 and 82029, were withdrawn on the last day of Southern steam - July 9 1967. No. 82027, a Bournemouth resident from January 5 until September 1964, was withdrawn in the week of January 8 1966, from Nine Elms.

Above: Low sun catches the side of 'T9' 4-4-0 No. 30310 as it approaches Ashley Heath with a train for Wimborne, where passengers for Bournemouth will have to change. No. 30310, a Bournemouth engine (from October 8 1957), was withdrawn from there in the week of May 30 1959, but the sole surviving 'Greyhound', No. 30120, is now at the Bluebell Railway.

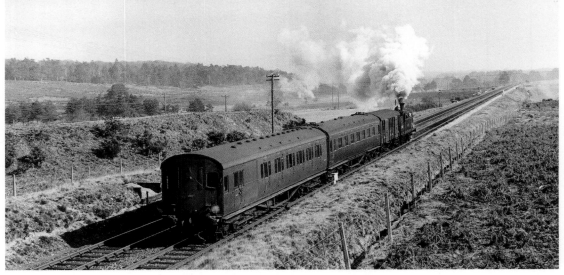

Above: An early 1960s picture, but one little-changed for years. An unidentified 'M7' 0-4-4T propels its Brockenhurst-Bournemouth 'push-pull' along the Ringwood line - colloquially known as 'Castlemans corkscrew'. The train has not long left the main line at Lymington Junction, just out of the picture to the right.

Above: A grey day, but a 'vintage' shot for me! This is Bournemouth 'Black Motor' No. 30695 shunting the small scrapyard at Ringwood in about 1957, before the pick-up goods duties were taken over by 'Q's. In the background, grounded bodies from some - even then - decidedly vintage cars await their end.

Above: 'West Country' No. 34006 *Bude*, one of three 'Light Pacifics' fitted with extended smoke deflectors (the others were Nos. 34004 *Yeovil* and 34005 *Barnstaple*), approaches Lymington Junction with a Waterloo-Bournemouth train in about 1961. Nine Elms shed, the 'Pacific's' home, has obviously taken good care of its charge, in contrast to a few years later when - whatever their pedigree - surviving locomotives were universally dirty. None of the locomotives with extended smoke deflectors survived; was withdrawn on March 19 1967.

Above: Bournemouth West was the usual terminus for Ringwood line trains. In this early 1960s view, rebuilt 'West Country' 4-6-2 No. 34001 *Exeter* waits to leave with a train for Waterloo, while grubby Standard '4MT' 2-6-0 No. 76056 simmers alongside. I think it is at the head of a Somerset and Dorset line train, which will take the Ringwood line as far as Broadstone, though these workings were normally entrusted to Eastleigh engines – home for No. 76056 was Bournemouth.

Below Left Opposite: A typical working for a Bulleid 'Pacific': rebuilt 'West Country' No. 34032 *Camelford* catches the early-morning sun as it potters away from Ringwood with a goods working at 7.15am in 1964. Shortly before, I had seen another 'Light Pacific' on this train in similarly mint condition so I think it may have been a running-in turn for Eastleigh works.

Above: A reminder that inclement weather in spring is not new! During the 'big freeze' a leaky 'M7', No. 30107, shrouds its train in steam as it crosses the largely frozen River Avon on the Ringwood line in March 1963. The bridge had been extensively strengthened the year before to allow the line's use as a relief route during electrification of the Bournemouth direct line, but barely another year was to pass before closure in 1964.

Right: The new 'corporate image' era is making itself felt, with the Southern Region green station nameboard having been replaced by a new black-on-white lower case example, as BR '4MT' 2-6-4T No. 80134 waits at Brockenhurst with a train for Lymington in 1966. Another sign of the modern age is the 'Hymek', rapidly approaching on the main line.
Today, Lymington is still served by trains from Brockenhurst, but the sidings in the background are long gone.

Above: Another early 1960s view - I think around 1962 - of Lymington Junction. One of the familiar LSWR 'M7' 0-4-4Ts, No. 30480, has just left the Lymington branch and heads for Brockenhurst. The old line via Ringwood diverges from the later main line behind the train to the right. No. 30480 was one of the 'X14' series of the Drummond 0-4-4Ts introduced in 1925 and fitted with 'auto' gear for 'push-pull' working, which can be seen mounted on the boiler and smokebox side.

Left: The Lymington branch trains had been the preserve of 'M7s' for years, but as they were withdrawn in the early 1960s other types came to be seen, including the relatively modern LMS-design Ivatt '2MTs'. In around 1963, No. 41310 (which has lost its shedcode plate) bustles along on a cold winter's day. The 'Mickey Mouse' tank has just joined the Ringwood line - Lymington Junction is around the bend out of sight to the right of the picture.

John L. Champion

■ What started your interest in railways?

I was born within sight of Wylde Green station, just along from Sutton Coldfield, and vaguely remember being held shoulder-high to watch trains. We took a holiday in Criccieth during 1934, when I was three. The journey, with a large-domed, long-chimneyed engine (a 'Duke' no doubt - I wonder which one?) and a view of the Cambrian from the guesthouse, are my first clear railway memories. Later that year we moved to Ealing, on the Great Western. During the war, we were evacuated to Northampton and a journey to visit my older brother in his Blackpool RAF quarters (behind 'Jubilees' Nos. 5556 *Novia Scotia* and 5571 *South Africa*) reawakened my interest.

■ How did you become interested in photography?

My first camera, a Coronet Cub, was a Christmas present in 1950. I later bought an Ensign Selfix which served me well for 12 years. In 1958 I started colour photography with a borrowed Paxette. I still use a Retinette that I bought in 1959. I tended to follow the approaches of P. Ransome-Wallis (get as good a picture as possible of a member of each locomotive class) and of H.C. Casserley and P.B. Whitehouse (concentrate on the older and smaller classes first and leave the rest until later).

■ Do you have any regrets?

This approach meant that, with engines disappearing so quickly, I missed some of the bigger stuff. My collection is sadly short of 'Pacifics' and 'Kings'.

■ Did you follow steam after 1968?

I moved to Gloucestershire in 1962, by which time we were seeing a rust bucket producing steam from all the wrong places. I gradually concentrated on industrial engines and the narrow gauge, visiting the Isle of Man in 1968 - the last year of the Peel and Ramsey lines. I enjoy preserved steam, but there's not the same 'ring' as before. I also enjoy road steamers.

Left: No self-respecting Gloucestershire enthusiast would fail to include a shot of the 'Chalford Flyer'. Collett 0-4-2T No. 1409 approaches Chalford with two autotrailers in tow in April 1963. The train has just passed a distinctive feature of the curving Golden Valley line - an especially tall signal, complete with back plate and situated on the 'wrong' side to aid sighting around bends.

Above: Early maths lessons: by counting wagons in freights just like this one as a young child in Ealing, I was able to reach 100 sooner than most of my schoolmates! This is Collett '2884' 2-8-0 No. 3853 (at this time allocated to Newport Ebbw Junction) passing Patchway on down coal empties on June 6 1961. The '2884' was a development of the original '28XX' with side window cabs and other detail differences.

Above: An immaculately turned out 'Jubilee', No. 45627 *Sierra Leone*, rolls past Midland Railway signals at Kettering with an express. The locomotive still carries the earlier BR emblem, though many of the coaches have by now been repainted from 'blood and custard' to maroon. This picture well represents my old 'stamping ground' and is typical of London Midland Region scenes of the late 1950s.

Above: The Meldon Quarry ballast workings were interesting from an engine-watcher's point of view. On July 9 1958 the train prepares to leave Exeter St David's, with no fewer than four locomotives. Polished lined-black 'M7' 0-4-4T No. 30023 pilots 'N' 2-6-0 No. 31841 and, in the distance, two 'E1/R' 0-6-2Ts are banking at the rear.

Above: My favourite picture, and the first taken on Kodachrome 2. Ex-Midland Railway '3F' 0-6-0 No. 43593 hauls a northbound train of empty mineral wagons, mostly of the BR variety, at Coaley Junction, Gloucestershire, in February 1962. Note the unusually (for this period) clean condition of the engine and immaculate track and fencing, which appear to have recently been renewed. Sadly, none of the class survived into preservation.

Right: Midland Railway '1P' 0-4-4T No. 58085 waits at Wellingborough on June 7 1952 with a Higham Ferrers push-pull train. The 15A shedplate shows it is allocated to Wellingborough. It was not withdrawn until April 1959, from Lincoln. The '1Ps' dated back to 1881, although No. 58085 was from an 1895 sub-class, and subsequently rebuilt with a Belpaire firebox. This was the first picture taken with my new Ensign Selfix camera. Note also the advertising poster and neat MR fencing.

Left: Opinions differ as to the most handsome locomotives to run in Britain, but to my eyes a well turned-out 'Castle' took a lot of beating. Here is No. 5094 *Tretower Castle* on the 'Cheltenham Spa Express' at Paddington on April 4 1959.

Above: The powerful lines of the rebuilt 'Royal Scot' 4-6-0s are evident in this study of Kentish Town's No. 46103 *Royal Scots Fusilier* at Kettering on the 2.25pm St Pancras train in September 1960. This train left Bradford at noon and on Saturdays was known as the 'Honeymoon Express'! 'Scots' were almost unknown on the Midland Main Line until West Coast electrification started in 1958, after which they were common until mid-1961. Kentish Town shed lost its last 'Scot' in October that year.

Standing under the trainshed at Euston, Caprotti 'Black Five' No. 44748 awaits departure with a train to the North. The 'Caprotti Fives' were introduced in 1948 and were easy to identify from their 'standard' classmates by the minimal running plate, splashers and prominent outside steam pipes. No. 44748 was withdrawn from Longsight (Manchester) in September 1964. No Caprotti 'Black Fives' survived into preservation.

Geoff Rixon

■ What started your interest in railways?

I suppose it all began with the launch of the Ian Allan ABCs. They came out during the war years which were pretty drab and I guess they gave me something to do. I'd had the typical schoolboy interest, with model train sets and suchlike. I grew up on the south-west side of London but was tempted with the LMS ABC so I went up to Willesden Junction and saw streamlined 'Duchess' No. 6237 City of Bristol, still in maroon.

■ What got you taking photographs?

During the war, I remember seeing aerial dogfights while going round Willesden sheds and thinking that I ought to record some of this. I bought a Box Brownie in 1947, although film was really hard to get hold of. It was ex-RAF reconnaissance film which was really sharp, providing the locomotive was stationary.

I then moved on to an Ensign Selfix 820 for black and white - which I left on a bus - and a Pentax S2 for 35mm colour. I started colour in 1959 with a trip to Scotland, using Kodachrome 10ASA film but then switched to 25ASA.

■ Where did you go?

Being a Londoner, I took a lot of photographs in London. We used to regularly visit Old Oak Common, Willesden, Neasden and Cricklewood sheds. We used to make friends by meeting people on the platform ends and so a group of us would get together and go off on tours of different parts of the country.

We'd save up for ages before setting off. However, you tended to get picky - these trips would be expensive so we'd choose where our favourite engines would be. We covered most of the country, but some places - particularly South Wales - would be a dead loss.

■ Do you have any regrets?

I really wish I'd started to take colour a couple of years earlier. If you look at colour taken in 1957, everything was still clean. But you get to 1959 and engines were really grubby. A lot changed between 1957 and 1959 and it made a big difference.

We go back to the era when steam was king in the capital city and its suburbs. Welcome to 'Steam in the smoke'. PICTURES BY GEOFF RIXON

Above: Two porters stop for a chat on Platform 10 of Brunel's famed Paddington station while Old Oak Common-based 'Castle' 4-6-0 No. 4082 *Windsor Castle* waits at the 'stops' on August 18 1962. The grubby 'Castle', which swapped its identity with No. 7013 *Bristol Castle* in 1952 to haul King George VI's funeral train, was withdrawn from Gloucester in the week of September 5 1964.

Right: In a scene full of 1960s atmosphere, grubby Drummond '700' 0-6-0 No. 30346, with just its number and crest cleaned, rolls through Woking with a down freight on July 20 1962. The '700s' and such wagons are now long gone from the national railway No. 30346 was withdrawn in the week of November 17 1962 from Feltham shed.

Above: Urie designed the class of five 'H16' 4-6-2Ts in 1921 specifically for use on interchange freight traffic between Feltham and Brent, and Feltham and Willesden. The class followed the outline of his bulky 'G16' 4-8-0Ts, built for Feltham 'hump' marshalling yard in July 1921. In June 1962, the fire glows in the cab of 'H16' No. 30518 as it passes through the cutting at Weybridge with a coal train from Feltham yard to Durnsford Road power station. No. 30518 was withdrawn from Feltham in the week of November 11 1962.

Left: Hauling a wonderful 'mixed bag' of SR, BR and LNER carriages and vans, the now-preserved but then very grimy 'Standard Five' 4-6-0 No. 73082 *Camelot* heads along the up slow line in the cutting near Weybridge in June 1962. *Camelot* entered traffic on June 24 1955 at Stewarts Lane and was withdrawn, after a working life of just 11 years, from Guildford on June 19 1966. Today, No. 73082 is preserved at the Bluebell Railway although its boiler ticket expired in 2005.

Above: Steam, smoke and grime... Rugby League Challenge Cup Final day brings Willesden shed to life with 'Jubilees', a 'Duchess' and an '8F' among other unidentified designs crowding in the smoky atmosphere. Stanier 'Jubilee' No. 45591 *Udaipur* and '8F' No. 48111 are the main identifiable locomotives on May 11 1963. No. 45591 was a Crewe North engine and No. 48111 was based at Nuneaton. Some new diesel locomotives can just be seen on the far left of the picture, bolstering steam for now, but soon to take over. No. 45591 was withdrawn in October 1963 although No. 48111 survived at Bolton until March 1968.

Right: Willesden 'Black Five' 4-6-0 No. 45111 runs through the approaches to Harrow and Wealdstone station with a fitted freight in June 1962 - ten years after the fatal crash when 112 people died there. The Stanier-designed 4-6-0 is heading south back to its home shed. It was based at Willesden between March 1962 and April 1963 when it moved to Chester London Midland shed. No. 45111 was withdrawn five years later in the week of October 28 1967 from Rose Grove (Burnley) and sent to Cashmore's of Newport for scrap.

Above: Beneath the canopy at Euston, Camden's Stanier 'Princess Coronation' 4-6-2 No. 46239 *City of Chester* draws a small audience while waiting for 'time' with a train to Liverpool in 1963. The 'Pacific' was just one year from retirement. No. 46239's final depot was Crewe North, where it had been based since the week of August 29 1964. It was withdrawn in the week of September 12 1964.

Right: Glistening in the sunlight at Paddington, GWR '94XX' 0-6-0PT No. 8433 is still in excellent external condition when photographed at the Western Region terminus in October 1963, after bringing in an empty stock working. But the end was on the horizon for No. 8433, with just two years to go before withdrawal on June 3 1965 after a period in store. The pannier's last shed was Old Oak Common.

Maurice Edwards

■ Maurice was introduced to railways by his father during the Second World War, when visits to Kilburn near Derby were rewarded with the sights of - amongst others - the 'Coronation Scot'.

■ An initial interest in photography came from a Kodak 'Box Brownie' camera "to take as many pictures as possible", later leading to a job as a Press Photographer in the mid 1950s.

■ Maurice's interest in railways picked up again in the early 1960s, by now using a 5x4 MPP Micro Press camera. He had three particularly favourite spots: the watertroughs at Bushey (West Coast Main Line), Hadley Wood North Tunnel (East Coast Main Line) and Sonning cutting (GW Main Line). He never stayed with one particular region - and covered all the former 'Big Four'.

■ Maurice Edwards has done a Glorious Years before (August/September 1994), but with such a wide range of interesting subjects we couldn't resist re-visiting his collection...

■ In SR287 we brought you the first part of Maurice Edwards' wonderful 'The Glorious Years' selection. There's such a wide variety of locomotive classes and areas in his archive that this issue we present a second selection.

■ Maurice never photographed the railway in just one region. He travelled over much of the network to take in the Western, Southern, Midland and Eastern Regions in the 1950s and early 1960s.

■ Maurice was introduced to railways by his father during the Second World War when visits to Kilburn near Derby were rewarded with the sight of the 'Coronation Scot'.

■ An initial interest in photography came from a Kodak Box Brownie camera "to take as many pictures as possible", later leading to a job as a press photographer in the mid-1950s.

■ In 1994 Maurice Edwards' work was featured in a two-part 'Glorious Years' (SR172/173).

Left: Racing along the Great Western main line, GWR 'King' 4-6-0 No. 6023 King Edward II is at the head of 'The Red Dragon' on July 5 1961 in Sonning Cutting. The four-cylinder Collett locomotive was built in 1930. Even 13 years after nationalisation, the 'Western' image is still very strong. No. 6023 was withdrawn on June 19 1962 from Cardiff Canton after 32 years in traffic.

Appropriately carrying full 'Golden Arrow' regalia, Stewarts Lane's 'Battle of Britain' 4-6-2 No. 34086 *219 Squadron* storms towards Shorncliffe with a London-bound working on May 22 1960. No. 34086 was built in 1948 and was at first allocated to Ramsgate. It was withdrawn after an 18-year career from Eastleigh.

STEAM RAILWAY

Right: Winding through the streets on Weymouth's famous tramway, an unidentified GWR '1366' 0-6-0PT takes a Paddington to Weymouth boat train down to the harbour in August 1952. Weymouth-based members of the class were regularly used on the characteristic tramway during the 1950s and carried a bell on the running board to warn pedestrians and cars of their approach. No. 1369 survives, at the South Devon Railway.

'Battle of Britain' 4-6-2 No. 34086 *219 Squadron* has charge of the empty stock move to Dover on May 23 1960 in readiness for that day's up 'Golden Arrow' working at Folkestone Junction. The empty stock was regularly worked to Dover tender first by the train engine before it returned to London.

Above: Painted in Great Eastern Railway Blue but, with BR crests, Liverpool Street station pilot 'J69' 0-6-0T No. 68619, has again been immaculately turned out on February 25 1961, when it simmers in the atmospheric station. Based at Stratford since before nationalisation, the diminutive Holden engine was withdrawn on October 30 1961. Sister 'J69' No. 87 (68633) survives at the National Railway Museum.

Above: With water pouring from the tender overflow, Stanier 'Black Five' No. 45134 races over the 'troughs' at Bushey - one of Maurice Edwards' favourite spots - on May 10 1960. The Crewe South-based LMS 4-6-0 is in charge of a northbound goods train. No. 45134 was withdrawn from Carnforth on August 3 1968 after 33 years in service.

Left: On a murky but atmospheric March 8 1960, Stanier 'Jubilee' No. 45694 *Bellerophon* starts out from St Pancras, with the 'Thames Clyde Express' to Glasgow. The Holbeck based 4-6-0 was built on March 25 1936 and first allocated to Crewe North shed. The 'Jubilee' ended its working days in the North West working from Wakefield, from where it was withdrawn on January 4 1967.

Left: Brighton -based LBSCR Billinton 'K'2-6-0 No. 32342 potters through Rye, on the former South Eastern and Chatham line from Ashford to Hastings, with a short goods bound for Hastings on February 28 1961. The class of 17 Brighton 'Moguls' was introduced in 1913 to haul the London Brighton and South Coast Railway heaviest goods trains. They were based at Brighton, Fratton and Norwood sheds. No. 32342 was withdrawn from Brighton on December 30 1962 - it had been based there since nationalisation apart from a two-day loan to Fratton depot in 1950. The 2-6-0 was cut up at Eastleigh.

Above: Leaning from a precarious position, one of the crew of Stroudley 'Terrier' No. 32678 turns the water on to fill the tanks of the 0-6-0T at Havant, in preparation for the next train to Hayling Island on June 19 1962. The Eastleigh-based 'Terrier' was built in 1880 and lasted in BR service until October 6 1963, before entering preservation. Today No. 32678 is in traffic at the Kent and East Sussex Railway, with KESR blue-liveried classmate No. 3 Bodium (No. 3670).

Right: Thompson 'L1' 2-6-4T No. 67731 propels a rebuilt Class 307 Electric Multiple Unit over the 'hump' at Goodmayes yard on March 13 1962. The L1 mixed traffic 2-6-4Ts were introduced in 1945. No. 67731 was taken into traffic on October 26 1948 at Hitchin, where it spent just a couple of months before transferring to Stratford on January 2 1949. It was withdrawn on September 16 1962, from Stratford.

Above: Ex-works duo: Even in 1962 Swindon works was still turning out pristine steam locomotives. On March 14, '28XX' 2-8-0 No. 2876 (allocated to Aberdare) stands alongside 'County' 4-6-0 No. 1021 *County of Montgomery* (from St Philips Marsh). The 2-8-0 was withdrawn from Newport Ebbw Junction in the week of December 26 1964. No. 1021 was withdrawn from St Philip's Marsh on November 11 1963.

Left: Stewarts Lane 'Battle of Britain' 4-6-2 No. 34089 *602 Squadron* drifts slowly through Ashford with the 2.30pm Victoria to Folkestone Boat Train on March 4 1961. No. 34089 was taken into traffic, in air-smoothed condition, on December 31 1948 at Ramsgate. The 'Battle of Britain' was rebuilt in November 1960 and lasted until the very end of steam on the Southern Region. It was withdrawn from Salisbury on July 9 1967.

Above: Top Link freight: A welcome breath of fresh air for the crew of Gresley 'A4' 4-6-2 No. 60025 *Falcon*, as the 'Pacific' storms out of Hadley Wood north tunnel with a northbound goods on April 5 1960. The 'A4', based at Kings Cross, 'top shed' spent its entire BR working life on the East Coast Main Line. It was based at Grantham and New England (Peterborough) depots as well as 'Top Shed' during its career, which ended on October 20 1963.

Below: With a long freight behind the tender, 'Hall' 4-6-0 No. 4987 *Brockley Hall* rumbles west along the Great Western Main Line in Sonning Cutting on July 5 1961. The Reading-based 'Hall' was already in its final year of operation. It was withdrawn on April 9 1962, from Southall.

James Aston

▪ What started your railway interest?

When I was a child, my family used to picnic beside the main line between Hampton Court Junction and Esher station, and my fascination stemmed from these visits. I was just a year old when the new 'Scotch Arthurs' were delivered - my mother always claimed that my first words were 'King Arthur' - but perhaps that's just a myth! When I was a little older, I used to sit in a willow tree alongside the line, overlooking Marsh Lane signalbox - a wonderful place from which to watch trains.

▪ So what drew you into photography?

I used to pick up railway magazines at WH Smith's bookstalls on stations as a child and gaze in awe at the wonderful pictures by people like Eric Treacy and C.C.B. Herbert. I soon longed to be able to take such pictures myself! My entry into photography actually came about in the aftermath of the war. Before the war, I'd worked for a shipping company, but was called up into the 14th Army, spending my time in the Far East. While in Upper Assam I borrowed a camera and took a few shots of standard British designs - and wartime American 'MacArthurs' - on the local shed. But it wasn't just the pictures - the whole railway experience has always excited me and I well remember the drama of travelling through India by train. But cameras were expensive, particularly for young men on limited means. Then on 'demob' in 1947 I spent my Army gratuity on a camera. It was a Super Ikonta and cost £64, second-hand. I still have it stored in a drawer at home - it's been through three sets of bellows, but it was the only camera I used for my black and white photography. However, I did later move to 35mm and colour transparencies for non-railway subjects.

▪ What was your approach to photography?

It changed over the years. At first I was keen to record a good picture of every Southern Railway class. My beloved SR always remained my main focus, although I also took the opportunity of visits to 'in-laws' in Penzance to photograph the Western Region. But with the publication of the Modernisation Plan in 1955, it became obvious that the branch lines were under threat - first from dieselisation, but very soon from complete closure. So I altered my style and started trying to capture the way of life of these lines before it was too late. My photography at London termini continued as before, however, mostly while on my way home from work.

▪ When did your 'Glorious Years' come to an end?

I didn't go out much in the last two years of Southern steam - mainly because the engines were in such a deplorable condition and because there were hundreds of other photographers all recording run-down Bulleid 'Pacifics' from every conceivable angle, so I didn't see a great deal of point! But I only completely packed in railway photography in 1972 when the '4 COR' electric units, which I remembered from my childhood (they were introduced in 1937), were finally withdrawn. Since then I've taken occasional pictures at preserved lines or of railways abroad, but not many.

▪ Do you have any regrets?

I suppose most people have at least some regrets - mine is that my photography tended to be fairly conservative. If I did it again, I'd like to think I'd be a little more adventurous in my approach. Another regret is that in a fit of patriotic fervour I gave up all my spotting notebooks for recycling in 1940, so I now have no record of what I saw before the war!

Left: In the years following the Modernisation Plan, I turned more to the branch line scene. This is South Easern and Chatham 'H' 0-4-4T No. 31263 (now preserved at the Bluebell Railway) running into Cranbrook with the 4.25pm for Paddock Wood on September 9 1960. A study in early-autumn light - though for so early in the evening it looks more like January than September! Why did so many 'H' firemen seem to fire as they ran into stations?

Above: The three remaining Beattie 'Well Tanks' were by the early 1960s favourites of fans of Southern steam, and were usually well turned out. Built in 1874 (though rebuilt at Eastleigh in 1921), '0298' No. 30585 potters through the woods near Penhargard, shortly after a water stop, on June 2 1960 with the 10.3am Wadebridge freight. No. 30585 survives at the Buckinghamshire Railway Centre, and the other survivor, No. 30587, is at the Bodmin and Wenford Railway.

Above: What a difference a few years make. Eleven years after nationalisation and steam has less than a decade to go. A rebuilt 'Merchant Navy' - all were altered between 1956 and 1959 - waits at Waterloo with the 6pm to Exeter. It is May 5 1959, and the 'Pacific' is No. 35009 *Shaw Savill*, which survives, although unrestored.

Bottom Left: Polished 'N1' No. 31879 waits at Cannon Street with a Derby Day Pullman special on May 30 1951. The bowler-hatted Inspector looks along the train for passengers - but there were hardly any. But then there was very little publicity. My firm had a box at Epsom and hired Daimler cars for themselves to go from the City. Fortunately they weren't tempted by the train or they might have wondered why I wasn't at my desk!

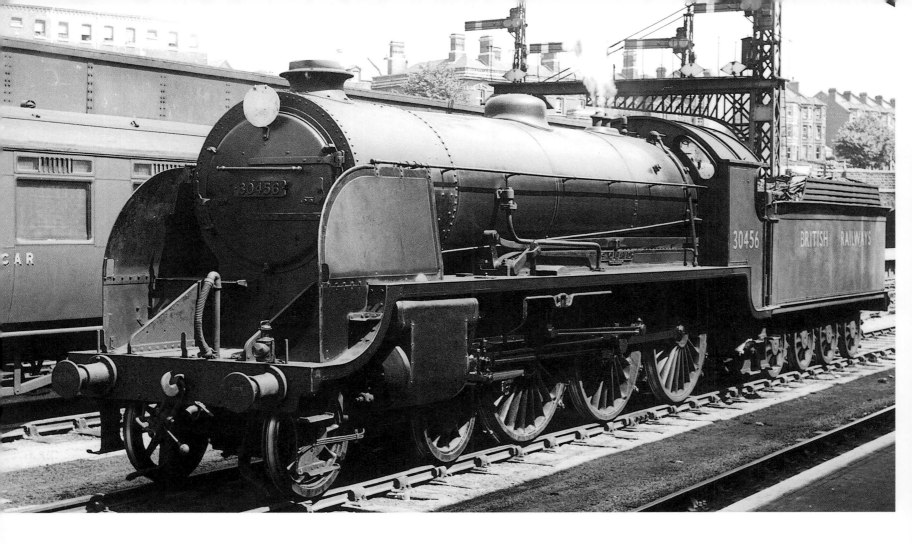

Above: Still in SR-style green, but with the new British Railways Gill Sans lettering and smokebox numberplate, 'King Arthur' No. 30456 *Sir Galahad* has just come off a down working at Exeter Central and waits for the 'dummy' to clear before it can sidle off to Exeter Junction shed. Pictured on July 9 1949, *Sir Galahad* still had almost 11 years to go before withdrawal, which came in the week ending May 14 1960. It was scrapped at Eastleigh the following week.

Right: The modernisation that nationalisation would bring is yet to come as South Eastern and Chatham Railway 'D' 4-4-0 No. 1748 simmers on shed at Ashford on May 8 1948 - the same day as the picture of *Bodiam* was taken (see page 135). The grubby black Wainwright engine is one of a class of thoroughbreds dating back to 1901, but has clearly seen better days. No. 1748 was scrapped, but of the 51 built, a solitary example, No. 31737 (SECR No. 737), survives at the National Railway Museum.

Above: Even the plain black livery adorning 'King Arthur' No. 800 *Sir Meleaus de Lile* looks attractive as the shiny 4-6-0 waits to leave Cannon Street with the 5.40pm train to Ashford on May 6 1949. It is a scene full of detail - on the tender the 'Southern' lettering from an earlier coat of paint is starting to show through, steam at the bufferstops betrays the presence of the engine used to bring in the empty stock, and Cannon Street's great glass-less roof soars overhead. In the background two electric units wait for passengers.

Left: A timeless scene as London and South Western Railway 'O2' No. W33 *Bembridge* runs into Wootton with the 10am Freshwater to Ryde on September 16 1953. It was a tight fit under the bridge for both of us! Happily steam still runs to Wootton, under the auspices of the Isle of Wight Steam Railway. *Bembridge* wasn't so lucky; being 'honourably discharged' on January 1 1967.

Above: A reminder of South London's steam scene in the early post-war years as 'King Arthur' No. 30452 *Sir Meliagrance* gets into its stride, passing Vauxhall on July 8 1950 with a down West of England train. Since its return to the 'third rail', steam can still be seen at this spot, but like all 'King Arthurs' except No. 30777 *Sir Lamiel*, No. 30452 succumbed to the torch, in this case following withdrawal in August 1959.

Above: The 6pm Plymouth train awaits departure from Waterloo on September 9 1948. 'Battle of Britain' *Sir Frederick Pile* illustrates well the SR/BR transition - carrying the Southern 'target' on the smokebox, but 'British Railways' on the tender and an 'S' prefix (to denote the region) to its Bulleid number 21C158. Built just the year before the picture was taken, the 'Pacific' was rebuilt in 1960 (by then as No. 34058), and is one of 20 'Light Pacifics' to survive.

Bottom Left: 'Pacific' tank No. 30519 has its smokebox cleaned at Feltham shed on April 4 1953. Robert Urie's five chunky 'H16s' were imposing locomotives - though this one seems to have been in a slight accident as it has a bent front bufferbeam. Designed for heavy freight traffic, the last 'H16' (No. 30517) was withdrawn in December 1962. No. 30519 was withdrawn in the week ending November 17 that year, though its final end came almost a year later when it was scrapped in October 1963.

Above: On a fine June 26 1948, 'King Arthur' No. 30744 *Maid of Astolat* calls at Tisbury on the London and South Western line with the 3.5pm slow train from Salisbury to Exeter Central. Although it is just six months after nationalisation, *Maid of Astolat* already carries its BR identity - though in Southern 'Sunshine' style complete with green smoke deflectors and shaded lettering, including the painted front number.

Above: The light railway lives on at Headcorn on May 8 1948 - the third anniversary of VE Day - as Kent and East Sussex Railway No. 3 *Bodiam* waits with the 12.35pm to Tenterden. The train was strengthened by an additional Brake Third coach, seemingly for a pair of grey-haired ladies who alighted from the 11.15am from Charing Cross. The already 76-year old No. 3 would soon become BR No. 32670, and remarkably more than half-a-century later survives on the KESR, restored to its *Bodiam* identity.

Bottom Left Opposite: On June 5 1958, 'King Arthur' No. 30806 *Sir Galleron* leaves Cannon Street with the 5.47pm for Dover. The bowler-hatted Station-master Gregory stood and watched as the immaculate 'N15' set off for the coast. They cared in those days! By this time the 'King Arthurs' were approaching the end of their careers, which had lasted more than three decades. The final shed for No. 30806 was Eastleigh, from which it was withdrawn in the week ending April 29 1961. It was cut up in June that year.

Peter Fitton

Peter, aged 60, works as an optician. He first started photographing steam in 1958 through the influence of local photographer Frank Dean and has a huge archive of pictures, both black and white and colour, dating to the present day.

Left: Powering up the grade from Bradford with the 8.20am to Bridlington on July 1 1967 comes Riddles 'Standard Five' 4-6-0 No. 73141. The '5MT' was one of 30 built with outside Caprotti valvegear. The rest of the class, which totalled 172 machines, had Walschaerts motion. No. 73141 was built in 1956 and lasted until July 29 1967, when it was withdrawn from Patricroft. Five of the class survive in preservation including No. 73129 (based at the Midland Railway - Butterley), the only Caprotti survivor. The last 'Caprotti Five' was returned to steam in 2005.

Right: Off the rails - Thompson 'B1' 4-6-0 No. 61306 (now preserved at the Nene Valley Railway and named 'Mayflower'), has run into grief in Laisterdyke yard on July 3 1967. The re-railing crew have arrived and set about getting the 71-ton locomotive back on the rails. The 'B1' was taken into traffic on April 5 1948 and spent the next 11 years based in Hull at both Dairycotes and Botanic Gardens sheds before moving to Low Moor in June 1967. After just three months at Low Moor No. 61306 was withdrawn on September 30 1967.

Below: The industrial system at Seaham Harbour was wonderfully atmospheric, with a character completely different to the 'big railway'. On July 7 1967, the ancient and work worn but purposeful looking Lewin 0-4-0ST No. 18 stands alongside a row of hoppers at the harbour. Then thought to have been built in 1863, but believed to date from 1877, the 0-4-0ST was eventually preserved in 1975 at the North of England Open Air Museum, Beamish. During No. 18's long career at Seaham it had been rebuilt twice. When it arrived at Seaham in 1899 the Poole-built engine was an 0-4-0WT. Rebuilt as a 0-4-0T it was rebuilt again in 1927, when it became an 0-4-0ST with outside cylinders. It is slowly being restored.

Above: No fewer than six 'Dub-dee' 2-8-0s can be glimpsed on shed at Normanton as a seventh former War Department locomotive, No. 90076, heads for the depot on July 4 1967. The 2-8-0 had been based on the London and North Eastern Railway and North Eastern Region since being released from WD service on November 28 1945. Its last depot was West Hartlepool, from where the 'Austerity' was withdrawn on September 9 1967. A former Swedish-based engine is under restoration at the Keighley and Worth Valley Railway and will eventually run as BR 'No. 90733'.

Above: Taking the right hand curve at Pleck Junction on August 21 1964, 'Super D' 0-8-0 No. 49407 leads Stanier 'Black Five' No. 44873 on a heavy freight train towards Wolverhampton. By now the grimy 'Super Ds' were the last representatives of the once proud London and North Western Railway. No. 49407 lasted until 1964, when it was withdrawn from Bescot. The then-Becsot allocated 'Black Five', was withdrawn on December 2 1967 from Wigan Springs Branch. Fortunately examples of both classes still exist.

Above: The traditional railway at work: 'Black Five' No. 44916 passes the magnificent mechanical signalbox at Manningham on June 7 1967. The parcels train hauled by the Stanier 4-6-0 is the 3.18pm Bradford-Heysham. No. 44916 was withdrawn in December the same year, from Stockport shed. It had spent 22 years in traffic. Doesn't this scene say volumes about a railway which has now almost completely vanished?

Bottom Left: With the mills so typical of the area forming a backdrop, Stanier two-cylinder 2-6-4T No. 42616 steams through the closed Laisterdyke station near Bradford on May 29 1967, with a train ultimately bound for Kings Cross. The Great Northern Railway's Laisterdyke (on the line from Bradford Exchange to Pudsey) opened in 1854. It had closed the previous summer, on July 4 1966. The train had originated at Bradford Exchange with the Low Moor-based locomotive taking charge on the first leg. The 1937-built '4MT' remained in service until September 30 1967, when it was withdrawn .

Above: How the railway has changed since this photograph was taken... an evocative portrait of Hughes/Fowler 'Crab' 2-6-0 No. 42754 at Ansdell and Fairhaven on the Kirkham-Blackpool Central line perfectly captures the atmosphere of the 1960s railway that was about to disappear. The Lower Darwen-based 2-6-0 had charge of the 12.45pm from Blackburn on March 7 1964, just eight months before it was withdrawn from Gorton, in the week of November 14 1964.

Above: Clear light at Carnforth on January 3 1967 highlights no fewer than 11 locomotives awaiting their next duties. Visible are 'Black Five' No. 45466 (allocated to Speke Junction), Fairburn 2-6-4T No. 42134 (Tebay) and 'WD' 2-8-0 No. 90721 (Normanton). Other - unidentified - locomotives represent classes including Stanier '8F' 2-8-0s, an Ivatt 'Flying Pig' 2-6-0 and a Riddles '9F' 2-10-0.

Bottom Left: Both Station and locomotive are no more... Thompson 'B1' No. 61030 *Nyala* powers up the steep grade out of Bradford Exchange with the 3.5pm to King's Cross on September 10 1966. The Wakefield-based 4-6-0 lasted until September 30 1967 when it was withdrawn from service from Low Moor. Happily, two Thompson 'B1s' survive in preservation: Nos. 61264 and 1306 'Mayflower', both of which are now operational.

Left: Riddles 'Britannia' 4-6-2 No. 70014 *Iron Duke* catches the late-afternoon light at Carnforth depot on January 3 1967. Even towards the end of its life (it was withdrawn from Carlisle Kingmoor on December 30 1967), the locomotive presents a modern, powerful impression - hardly surprising for an engine only built in 1951. During its short life, the 'Pacific' was allocated to no fewer than 14 depots including Stewarts Lane, Norwich, Willesden and Llandudno Junction.

Below: In the work-worn condition sadly so typical of the last years of steam, 'Black Five' No. 45295 hammers through Stricklands, near Shap on the West Coast Main Line on August 19 1967. The Stanier 4-6-0 is in charge of train 1M21 from Glasgow to Blackpool North, which is made up of a mixed rake of coaches also typical of the 'transition period'. In the train are a maroon LMS Stanier brake, and both blue-and-grey and maroon Mk 1s. The locomotive was now nearing the end of its career - it lasted until December 1967 when it was withdrawn from Carlisle Kingmoor after 31 years' service.

Right: 'How many did you say it was hauling?' Riddles '9F' No. 92233 justifies its massive haulage capacity with an enormous rake of Mk 1 coaches at Charnock Richard on the West Coast Main Line on August 23 1967. The train was a 'down' empty coaching stock move. The 2-10-0 was just 10-years old when it was withdrawn from Speke Junction in the week ending February 3 1968.

Below: 'Tanks' on the move: there weren't many locomotives that Rose Grove's 'Jinty' 0-6-0T No. 47211 could dominate, but Lostock Hall's tiny '0F' 0-4-0ST No. 47008 is one of them. The cheeky-looking pair accelerate away from Preston and along the main line on March 11 1964. Despite appearances, No. 47008 was a modern engine - it was built in 1953 and spent its working life allocated to Preston and Lostock Hall before withdrawal in the September after the picture was taken. One hopes that the chalked 'tank empty' on the side of No. 47211 wasn't accurate...

Keith Lawrence

■ **Age: 68**

■ **What started your interest in railways?**
My grandmother lived next to East Ardsley station on the LNER main line to Leeds. When I stayed there as a small boy I would watch the trains go past, including 'The West Riding Limited'. Nothing remains of the vast yards, station, houses and locomotive depot, just the usual abandoned wilderness of modern railways. I had been to the Battle of Britain Airshow at Biggin Hill and had half a roll of film left in the camera which I had borrowed from a friend. I went up to my local railway line at Walton-on-Thames to finish it off. I started to investigate this dearth of steam and found out it was disappearing from our railways very quickly. I bought a camera of my own and set out to photograph what I could of what was left.

■ **When did your Glorious Years come to an end?**
They haven't really ever ended. After my last BR photographs I started to travel to the Continent to photograph the railways there. Germany was a very good place for steam and I also caught some of the remaining French steam around Boulogne and in Paris. I worked for BEA, so when BEA and BOAC amalgamated, this allowed me to travel worldwide to catch the steam scene. As recently as last August I was up at Fort William to photograph and travel on 'The Jacobite' hauled by LNER 'K1' No. 62005. I would heartily recommend this trip to anyone who needs a steam fix!

Left: After a century of service the end of Southern steam is signalled as BR 'Standard 5' No. 73119 *Elaine* **passes Walton-on-Thames in March 1967. The picture must have been taken before March 19 when the 4-6-0, new to Nine Elms on December 9 1955, was withdrawn from Eastleigh.**

Above: Guildford's last day - July 9 1967 - saw the end of steam on the Southern and the emptying of the shed too. The half-roundhouse already appears empty inside although two locomotives are still in steam outside. Guildford started 1967 with 13 working steam locomotives. Among the last to leave were 'USA' 0-6-0T No. 30072, on the turntable, and 'West Country' No. 34018 *Axminster* (on the right with its nameplates removed). BR 'Standard Five' No. 73029 passes the shed with an up train before entering the station. All three locomotives in this photograph were withdrawn that day - only No. 30072 was based at Guildford.

Above: Stanier '8F' No. 48727 rolls towards to Accrington with a mixed freight on August 1 1968. The painted smokebox numberplate shows that the souvenir hunters have already been busy, though someone has also taken the effort to clean the Stanier engine. The Rose Grove 2-8-0 was withdrawn two days later, after 24 years work with the LMS and BR. But on this day at least the railway scene at Accrington is still as it should be...

Bottom Left: 'The end'. BR '5MT' No. 73093 stands at Basingstoke on July 9 1967, the last day of steam on the Southern. After this date the increasingly desperate hunt for steam turned to the North West. No. 73093 had seen use on both the Midland and Western Regions before moving to the Southern, but for the Riddles engine this was the end of the road.

Above: With a day to go before steam finished on BR, Carnforth's 'Standard 4' 4-6-0 No. 75048 passes Silverdale 'box in North Lancashire in charge of a short freight working. This was August 2 and within 24 hours the 4-6-0 was withdrawn. It was sent for scrap at Campbell's of Airdrie.

Above: Steam comes to an end, but 'Pompey' carries on... For the author of the chalk markings, the performance of Portsmouth Football Club is obviously as important as mourning the end of Southern steam. BR 'Standard Five' No. 73029 waits at Guildford with the very last steam-hauled train from Fratton - an empty stock working to Clapham Junction. The 4-6-0's fire was dropped for the last time that day at Nine Elms and it was assigned to the scrap line. It was sent to Cashmore's of Newport for scrap.

Above: A volcanic exhaust highlights the effort of Stanier '8F' No. 48410 on the climb to Copy Pit summit as the 2-8-0 drags a mineral train towards Todmorden. This was April 1967 - and partnering No. 48410 was another '8F' at the rear.
Springs Branch-allocated No. 48410 was withdrawn in the last week of steam.

Left: After visiting Eastleigh Works on August 23 1956 I saw 'M7' No. 30378 on a rake of ancient stock at the station. Apart from liveries, little had changed in this scene in years, though the Eastleigh allocated 0-4-4T to has at some time had its smokebox wing-plates and splasher-mounted sandboxes removed. Now all this is just a memory.

Left: By 1960, my signalman friend from St Ives had moved to Chesterton Junction (Cambridge) and this picture was taken during a trip to see him on September 24. Filthy 'J15' 0-6-0 No. 65457 - a member of a class going back to 1883 - arrives on the line from St Ives with a goods train. Note the collection of vans and wagons in the train, including a horsebox immediately behind the engine.

Hugo Appleton

▌ Your pictures cover a wide geographical area. Why is that?
I tended to take railway holidays around the country, often with friends, and many of the photographs stemmed from these trips. One of the largest was a tour round the South of England in the summer of 1956. We took in Ashford, Eastleigh, Southampton (including the Docks), the Isle of Wight, Exeter and Exmouth Junction on the Southern, returning on the Western via Newton Abbot, Bristol, Bath and Swindon - including a visit to the Works. In 1957, I visited my aunt and uncle in North Walsham, Norfolk and photographed the local network, and in 1961 a friend and I did North Wales, including trips to the slate quarries and the newly revived Talyllyn and Ffestiniog railways - as well as BR's Vale of Rheidol.

▌ Your pictures include some industrial views - were you particularly interested in industrial working?
I started getting into industrial steam in 1957-59 during my two years in the Army when I went to Stephson Locomotive Society meetings in Cambridge and met people who had an interest. While visiting North Walsham in 1957, I borrowed a bike and cycled to Wissington Sugar Beet factory. Then I did the Welsh slate quarries in 1961.

▌ Most pictures seem to have been taken on holidays. Didn't you take pictures at other times, even - as you were a railwayman - during the day?
No, I didn't tend to take anything during the week - or even very much at weekends. But this did start to change as more and more started to disappear in the 1960s.

▌ What started your interest in railways?
My grammar school at Huntingdon overlooked the station at Huntingdon North, and we could also see Huntingdon East, which at the time I started there (1947) had a 'J15' sub-shedded from Cambridge. We used to enjoy seeing it shuffling back and forth, on trains or shunting. In my last year of school a railway club was started (I became Secretary), and we visited great places like Stratford and Doncaster. Then, in August 1953, I joined the railway at Derby Works on an engineering apprenticeship. It was still overwhelmingly steam-oriented then and I worked on building the new BR 'Caprotti Fives'. After I finished my apprenticeship in 1959, I started two years' deferred National Service, ending up at the Longmoor Military Railway. After being demobbed, I returned to British Railways and rose through the engineering ranks before retiring, from Derby, in 1996.

▌ How did you become interested in photography?
I had a folding 'Brownie' from school days but wanted something better, and after I had been working for two years bought a Voigtlander 'Bessa I'. I still have it as a memento, but I subsequently bought another Voigtlander, a 'Contessa'. During National Service at Longmoor, I was a member of the camera club and experimented with colour film.

▌ Do you have any regrets?
I wish I'd taken more photographs when the opportunity was there!

▌ Did you follow steam after 1968?
Not really; I basically gave up in the mid-1960s, although I still made an effort for special events. I also photographed the preserved main line steam that came to Derby in the 1980s and early 1990s - my office overlooked the siding on which the locomotives were serviced.

Above: A pal of mine was a signalman at St Ives Junction and this picture was taken during a visit to see him, while I was on leave from the Army during my National Service. Riddles '2MT' 2-6-0 No. 78020 - the BR development of the original LMS version - stands alongside the signalbox with (I think) a train from Kettering to Cambridge on June 6 1959.

Above: Trips to North Walsham gave the opportunity to visit the Midland and Great Northern Joint line, which ran parallel to the Great Eastern for a short way. 'Flying Pig' 2-6-0 No. 43091 heads south towards Honing with a train for Yarmouth on July 17 1957. The modern Ivatt 'Mogul' - a type strongly associated with the M&GN - contrasts starkly with the train's old wooden-bodied stock.

Far Left: I had relatives in North Walsham and during a visit in 1957 took the opportunity to photograph the local lines. This is 'D16/3' No. 62586, at the time a Norwich engine, having been transferred there the previous month. The locomotive was a Gresley rebuild with round-topped firebox of the earlier 'D15', itself a Belpaire firebox development of the original Great Eastern Railway 'Claud Hamilton'. The 4-4-0 is making good progress between North Walsham and Worstead on July 17 1957 - I think with a Cromer to Norwich train.

Left: Hunslet 0-4-0ST No. 409 *Velinheli* shunts at Dinorwic Quarry on June 20 1961. The locomotive, built without a dome but fitted with one by the 1930s, is now at the Launceston Steam Railway in Cornwall.

Below: Derby Works apprentices looked forward to the two day 'September Break', granted *in lieu* of days worked earlier in the year. During that break on September 20 1956 the East Coast Main Line of the era is perfectly represented as 'A3' No. 60051 *Blink Bonny* roars through Abbots Ripton, the 'West Riding' headboard proudly displayed. At this time the 'Pacific' was allocated to Copley Hill.

Below : More memories of the Great Eastern as grimy inside-cylinder 'B12' 4-6-0 No. 61542 heads a train of 'blood and custard' Mk 1s between North Walsham and Worstead, on July 17 1957. No. 61542 is now long gone, having been withdrawn on July 14 1959, but classmate No. 61572 is based just a few miles away at the North Norfolk Railway.

Right: Taken during a holiday in 1956, this is Adams 'Radial' No. 30583 leaving Axminster for Lyme Regis on August 27. The wonderful 1885-built 4-4-2T was one of three '0415s' retained for working the Lyme Regis branch, and is the only one to survive into preservation. It is now on the Bluebell Railway.

Above: Hunslet 0-4-0ST *Linda* at Port Penrhyn, on June 19 1961. Penrhyn quarry closed in 1963 and Linda, together with classmate *Blanche*, ended up on the Ffestiniog Railway. There it remains today, modified with a tender as a 2-4-0STT. This picture, though, shows well the classic Penrhyn profile before the alterations, complete with a bucket on the bufferbeam holding sand. Classmate *Charles* is still in original condition, displayed at Penrhyn Castle museum.

Above: Gresley 'A4' 4-6-2 No. 60009 *Union of South Africa* at Little Ponton with the up 'Elizabethan' on August 23 1961. This was the last year of the 'non-stop' before 'Deltic' diesels took over on the East Coast Main Line, and 'Number 9' - the long-time Edingburgh Haymarket engine - was reallocated to Aberdeen. The 'Pacific' is once again a regular mainline performer.

Above: 'Britannia' No. 70040 *Clive of India* starts away from Huntingdon North with a southbound train on a bright, cold day in 1961. Although the 'Pacific' is grimy and leaking steam, someone has made the effort to pick out the smokebox hinges and other details in white paint - including the 40B shedplate, showing that the '7MT' is allocated to Immingham.

Above: Unique BR '8P' 4-6-2 No. 71000 *Duke of Gloucester* poses at Derby Works open day in August 1960. By this time the 'Pacific', built at Crewe just six years before as a replacement for the wrecked No. 46202 *Princess Anne*, was already being made obsolete by dieselisation. Just two years later it was withdrawn, on November 24 1962. Four decades later, the 'Duke' is.

Above: In a view taken from the last wagon, hard-working Hunslet 0-4-0ST *Linda* hauls a Penrhyn Quarry Railway slate train bound for Port Penrhyn on June 29 1961. By the time of this picture, taken while on holiday with a friend, the 1893-built saddle-tank was already 68 years old.

Above: Vale of Rheidol 2-6-2T No. 9 *Prince of Wales* waits at Aberystwyth on June 23 1961. Although the railway survives today, this scene is no more. The Vale of Rheidol's line was rerouted into the standard gauge station, using the former bay platforms, at Aberystwyth in 1968 and the original terminus closed (see SR253). The locomotives have also been modernised: No. 9 is now oil-fired and air-braked. In addition, its profile has been altered with the fitting of a taller cab and chimney, and changes to the shape of its bufferbeam.

Left: Locomotive crews greet each other as an unidentified Ivatt '2MT' 2-6-0 enters Pantydwr station (between Llanidloes and Builth Wells) with a southbound train for Brecon in June 1960, rolling past a train heading north. Note also the neatly kept platform and siding.

Above: Ivatt '2MT' 2-6-0 No. 46526, at Three Cocks Junction in June 1960, attracts attention from potential passengers. Apart from the grubby 'Mogul', little has changed in this scene since pre-Nationalisation days - from the GWR coaches which No. 46526 is hauling, to the neatly painted fire buckets hanging from the signalbox. The engine was at this time allocated to Oswestry.